T0265570

Confessions of a
Home Army Executioner

CONFESSIONS OF A HOME ARMY EXECUTIONER

A Memoir of the Polish Home Army

STEFAN DĄMBSKI

Preface by Teresa Dambski Ponce De Leon

Forewords by Roger Moorhouse and Zbigniew Gluza

Translated and Introduced by Marek Sobieralski

Greenhill Books

Confessions of a Home Army Executioner

Greenhill Books

Original Polish language *Egzekutor* published by Fundacja Ośrodka KARTA
First published by Greenhill Books, 2024
Greenhill Books, c/o Pen & Sword Books Ltd,
George House, Unit 12 & 13, Beevor Street, Off Pontefract Road,
Barnsley, South Yorkshire S71 1HN

For more information on our books, please visit
www.greenhillbooks.com, email contact@greenhillbooks.com
or write to us at the above address.

CIP data records for this title are available from the British Library

ISBN 978-1-80500-028-0

The front cover of this English-language edition is based on the original
Polish-language edition, designed by Agnieszka Warda in 2020.
Jacket photographs © Family archive/Ośrodek KARTA

Typeset by JCS Publishing Services Ltd
Typeset in 12.5/18pt Adobe Caslon Pro
Printed and bound in Great Britain by CPI Group (UK) Ltd,
Croydon, CRO 4YY

Reviews for *Confessions of a Home Army Executioner*

This book is moral dynamite. It reveals not only what men can do in war but also what war can do to men. Its author, the 'Executioner', killed hundreds of people, both enemies and compatriots. At the end, disgusted, he was not the only person caught up in war to ask: Am I a murderer?

Norman Davies, historian, writer and respected academic specializing in the history of Europe, Poland and the UK.

This is a harrowing but important book. Written by Polish Home Army veteran Stefan Dąmbski and now excellently translated into English by Marek Sobieralski, this memoir records a rapid journey of a fresh-faced teenager into a seasoned executioner. This is also a moral tale of how war can corrupt and how, even justified, resistance can produce moral dilemmas.

The Polish Underground was a formidable organization and was the largest resistance movement in occupied Europe. It was unique in that it comprised both a military wing, Armia Krajowa or Home Army, as well as a civilian support network that filled the educational and social welfare void resulting from the Nazi occupation. During this occupation, Home Army courts passed death sentences on a variety of particularly unpleasant SS or Wehrmacht soldiers and functionaries. More controversially, similar sentences were passed on a number of Polish-born and *Volksdeutsche* civilians who had collaborated with the enemy. Although the vast majority of Poles resisted the Nazis in any way they could, enemy occupations always throw up opportunists who can turn on their neighbours for a bribe or wish to settle old scores. Dąmbski was one of the few AK members who volunteered to carry out these death sentences and therefore his memoir provides a rare chance to examine the mind of an 'executioner'.

This is not an easy read – the slaughter of both men and women is unremitting. And when the Nazis retreat before the end of the war, the Poles are forced to endure another occupation, this time by the Soviet Red Army. The executioner's skills are called for again, and Dąmbski willingly obliges.

In later life, Dąmbski blamed his role as executioner on his fervent adherence to his motherland. He claims that a deprived childhood and the pre-war climate of Polish nationalism prompted him to carry out his role with such zeal. Yet the reader is left with the feeling that the more targets he killed, the less sensitized he became and indeed, at times, he relishes his role. In the end, dispatching men and women who were deemed enemies of the cause becomes routine. In later life he made a confession, of sorts, for the brutality he had meted out during the war, and when he received a terminal cancer diagnosis in 1993, he killed himself, perhaps in the same calculating way.

Such is the secret nature of clandestine warfare that most of the incidents he describes cannot be corroborated. However, few would willingly boast of such bloody excesses and Dąmbski has left us with an unusual and extraordinary testimony of what enemy occupation can do to a people. Indeed, in occupied territories across the world today, his role is far from redundant.

Jonathan Walker, military history author and lecturer, and regular contributor to BBC radio and television documentaries.

This is a remarkable, and historically valuable, memoir about an extremely brutal series of events which are still largely unknown outside Poland. It exposes the dark realities of life in Poland under German, then Soviet, occupation and the predicament faced by the Underground Home Army in trying to fight its way to national independence. Highly recommended.

Roger Moorhouse, historian and author specializing in modern German and Central European history, with particular interest in Nazi Germany, the Holocaust and the Second World War.

Stefan Dąmbski in the Western occupation zone in Germany, 1947.
He is wearing the uniform of a Labor Service Company
of the US Army.

A smiling thirteen-year-old Stefan Dąmbski
in 1938, with no inkling of the upcoming war.

Contents

Foreword by Roger Moorhouse

O N   T H E   E V E N I N G   O F   1 September 1943, a three-man hit squad of the Polish Underground entered a Warsaw bar. Their prey that night was Lolek Skosowski, a local collaborator who had been passing information to the Gestapo, and – for his pains – had been sentenced to death in absentia by the Underground. Skosowski, who had been lured to the bar on the premise of a meeting, was quickly dispatched with three pistol shots to the head. By the time the police arrived, thirty minutes later, the executioners were long gone; only the body of Skosowski remained, as a reminder to others not to collaborate with the Gestapo.

The wartime Polish Underground was exceptional in German-occupied Europe. For those in the English-speaking world who were raised on stories of the bravery of the French Maquis, the assumption is often made – subconsciously or not – that the French resistance represented something of a benchmark, a standard by which others would be judged. However, by all available measures, the Polish Underground exceeded that standard. It was more populous, more effective and more thoroughgoing, representing not just a resistance force but an underground state, with government ministries and official bodies, as well as a functioning judiciary and a military arm, all operating in a clandestine manner beneath the very jackboot of the German occupation. The Maquis, in comparison, seems like child's play.

Given the necessary scope of clandestine activity in occupied Poland, and the extremely brutal conditions in which they were operating, it should come as no surprise that the Polish Underground had teeth. The primary organization charged with executions was known as the Kedyw, the 'Directorate of Diversion', which was responsible for sabotage actions and reprisals, as well as the elimination of collaborators and Nazi personnel. The scale was nothing if not ambitious. In all, it is thought that the Polish Home Army planned as many as 5,733 assassinations,* ranging from the lowliest collaborator, like Skosowski, to the SS and Gestapo chief of Warsaw, Franz Kutschera, who was ambushed on a Warsaw street in February 1944.

Unsurprisingly, perhaps, the story of the Polish Underground's executioners – like that of the wider wartime Underground – was for a long time hidden from view in the post-war period. The Underground was brutally persecuted by the Soviets after the war, with many prominent Home

---

* Norman Davies, *Rising '44*, (London, 2003), p. 197.

Army leaders being executed by the communist authorities. For the lower ranks, imprisonment was common if they were caught, so the majority went into exile or – if they remained in Poland – kept their mouths firmly shut about their wartime activities, in many cases taking their stories to their graves. It was only really after 1989, then, with the collapse of the communist regimes across central Europe, that the true story of the wartime Underground could finally begin to be told.

It is in this context that this book should be welcomed and recognized for the remarkable testimony that it is. Stefan Dąmbski was not a prominent executioner, indeed he came to the task only by volunteering to do a dirty job that no one else appeared to want. Also, operating in the south of Poland, near Rzeszów, he was far from the capital and from those that might have recorded his actions for posterity. Consequently, his is a strangely parochial tale, of rural priests, local toughs and of low-level, petty collaborators. As such, it was a world away from the high-stakes actions that took place in Warsaw, but it was no less horrific.

In retrospect, at least, Dąmbski was troubled by the horror. As he mentions in his conclusion to this memoir, he took on an 'animal-like state' as a young man, carrying out actions that the civilized world 'equated with murder'. Yet, for all that later remorse, his record of the actions in which he was involved portrays him as a cold killer, a man almost entirely lacking in empathy, and willing to carry out any act ordered by his superiors in the name of Poland. 'It was our duty', he wrote, 'to show the world that a Pole … will die with a smile on his face, "for your freedom and ours".'

Volumes have been written about the barbarization of warfare, and this episode too could be harnessed to illustrate that point: how ordinary men are brutalized by war and then brutalize others in their turn. However, there is a rather more nuanced point to make. Our assumption is often that the Second World War had – broadly – the same tone and character, whether it was fought in northern France, or in Italy, or in eastern Poland. But this would be erroneous. As countless examples have shown, there was very obviously a 'Western War', in which the rules of warfare were broadly followed, and the Germans treated their enemies – on the whole – with a modicum of decency, and an 'Eastern War' in which none of those niceties applied. The example of the infamous massacre at Oradour-sur-Glane in 1944 is instructive here. That massacre – in which 643 French civilians were murdered – was carried out by the SS *Das Reich* Division, which had just been transferred west from fighting the Soviets on the Eastern Front. It is often touted as being somehow universally emblematic of Nazi barbarism, but it is really notable only for its exceptionalism. Such things – though hideously commonplace in the eastern half of Europe – were really rather rare in the western half. In Poland, Ukraine and Belarus, every other village and town witnessed its own Oradour.

FOREWORD BY ROGER MOORHOUSE

This memoir, then, is – on one level at least – a reminder of that barbarism; of that murderous tone that the war assumed in its 'eastern' variant; it was dog eat dog, every man for himself, kill or be killed. The Polish Underground army, in trying to maintain even the idea of an independent Poland, while assailed by the murderous precepts of not one totalitarian ideology but two, was perhaps uniquely exposed to all the barbarism that the war in Europe had to offer. Occupied Poland, after all, was no stranger to the Holocaust, to mass deportations, reprisal killings and to ethnic cleansing: one in five Poles were killed in the Second World War, and many hundreds of thousands of its citizens were deported by the Soviets to Siberia for hard labour. For those shocked by Dąmbski's conduct, therefore, it is worth reminding ourselves of the horrors that he perceived himself as fighting against.

And fight them he certainly did. As is recounted here, Dąmbski participated in actions not only against the Germans and those who collaborated with them, but also against the Ukrainians in their bloody squabble with the Poles, and against the incoming Soviets in 1944 and 1945. It is a reminder that Poland did not face a single enemy during the Second World War; rather it was assailed from all sides, inhabiting a hostile environment of colliding totalitarian ideologies, and of conflicting national ambitions, all of which were exacerbated, aggravated and metastasized by circumstances.

On a human level, meanwhile, this remarkable book reminds us how far an ordinary individual can go while still convincing themselves that what they are doing is right and justified. It is significant, I think, that in later life Dąmbski came to question the utility of all that violence; how it left a 'bad taste' in his mouth, and was difficult to 'square with his conscience'. This is understandable, and speaks of a man who, for all the violence he experienced – and inflicted on others – never entirely lost his humanity. As such, his story is instructive for wider swathes of history, way beyond the comparatively narrow world of wartime central Europe. It is a reminder that few of those who commit atrocities in wartime are psychopaths; rather they are ordinary people enabled and encouraged to do things that – in calmer times – they would find unconscionable. In that, the book's message, and its warning, is universal.

Roger Moorhouse
2023

Foreword by Zbigniew Gluza

PRESENTED HERE IS THE real and shocking testimony of an individual who stood in the ranks of the Armia Krajowa, the Polish Home Army and found himself in the role of an ideological executioner. The author could have presented himself as a hero of the battles against the occupier, ready to give up his life for his country. Yet, another reason for his writing turns out to be self-accusation, and the desire to question heroism as such. He asks in his text if he became a murderer. Irrespective of the answer, the message presented to us is very much anti-war.

A faded, nearly 177-page computer printout – the only surviving example of this record – arrived at the KARTA Foundation in 2005, having been in the possession of Dąmbski's niece and nephew, Krystyna Dąmbska-Nichols and Aleksander Dąmbski. The memoir has no conclusion, and stops mid-sentence. The executioner's suicide in Miami, Florida, on 13 January 1993 prevented the completion of the work. However, it comes across as complete, just finishing somewhat abruptly at the end.

It is essential to understand who Stefan Dąmbski was in this account of his teenage years. He was born on 3 December 1925, in Nosówka, a village in the Subcarpathian province, in south-eastern Poland. It lies approximately 11 kilometres west of the regional capital Rzeszów. He was 16 years old when he joined the Armia Krajowa in 1942. And he was not yet 20 when in July 1945, he was in one of the first transfers to the West of exposed soldiers from his unit. He committed his memories to paper over the last dozen or so years of his life as a fully mature man capable of objectively looking at his own experience.

The author's life after the war was not easy. His family was scattered – Stefan's mother (who ran the estates of Nosyce and Dylągówka) had already died in 1934. His father, Count Kazimierz Dąmbski, did not focus on his sons, leaving for Colombia in the spring of 1939. During 1947–52 he was the editor-in-chief of *Nowy Dziennik* in New York.

Brothers Stefan and Stanisław were in the care of an unmarried aunt after their mother's death and were split up after the war. Stefan served in a US Guard Company near Nuremberg after ending up in the Western occupation zone, and played soccer professionally during the latter part of the 1940s. Stanisław was arrested by the Urząd Bezpieczeństwa (National Security Agency) in connection with Stefan's escape from Poland. He died of tuberculosis at the age of 26, after being released from prison in 1948.

In 1950, with the help of his father, Stefan emigrated to the United States, where he initially lived in Chicago, then in

Miami from 1976. He seems to have been somewhat rootless, undertook ad hoc unqualified work – in transport and trade – and changed jobs often. He was married three times. His daughter from his second marriage lives in the USA.

In 1975, Stefan Dąmbski visited Poland, where he saw his cousin Alexander in Silesia. He flaunted his American successes while at the same time fearing arrest in Poland. He started writing down his memories in the 1970s, and it must have been a slow process. He was still finishing them when he was terminally ill with cancer. In 1993 he killed himself by shooting himself in the head. His wife brought the urn with his ashes from the USA in 1994, and the local community bade farewell to him as if he was a hero. He was buried in Hyżne, Rzeszów County, in the family chapel, Kaplica Jędrzejowiczów.

In this memoir, Stefan is clearly not trying to put up a monument to himself – in many places, his words simply become a bitter confession. What was he writing for? Apparently, it was partly because he disagreed with the widespread image of military heroism. It was also from a sense of guilt – as strongly supported by his family – that he had killed so many people. He had mainly killed after receiving orders, but sometimes in the absence of clear orders, or even sometimes entirely by chance. He could remain, like others, behind the comfortable façade of heroic actions and hardships endured without making his doubts known. He wrote, however, in the belief that war should be a warning, rather than an incentive for heroism.

CONFESSIONS OF A HOME ARMY EXECUTIONER

The only passages that are omitted here are those not directly related to the described actions, repetitions, or somewhat too distant digressions. The omissions are noted. The rough and rather hasty entries required some editorial attention, but the whole work is strictly original. It seems that Stefan Dąmbski wrote convinced that he would leave a testimony of historical importance.

In a country whose official representatives praise the wartime mobilization of patriotism, the confessions of a teenager sent with weapons to kill mercilessly can perhaps help restore the balance. It is worth remembering that war is pure evil.

Zbigniew Gluza
KARTA Foundation
March 2020

Preface

Y FATHER, STEFAN DĄMBSKI, was a war hero as well as my personal hero. He was very proud of being Polish, and for that reason, he despised 'Polack' jokes. At the age of 16, he joined the Polish resistance and acted as an executioner, carrying out death sentences delivered by the Underground courts. He never expected to live through the war, and his early life was filled with tragedy.

He lost his mother when he was about 9 years old. He told me that he blamed himself for her death because he was always getting in trouble (as kids do) and she would say, 'You'll be the death of me yet.' His sister did not survive infancy, being only 4 years old when she died, and his brother died at age 25 after being imprisoned by the secret police.

During the war, death was all around him, too. His best friend was shot right next to him while they were in a ditch, fighting the enemy. My father was shot in the leg in the same battle, but that did not stop him from helping to carry his friend's body back to their unit and making sure he was properly buried.

My father's grandfather was a Polish count, and he grew up in a forty-six-room castle. The family went from that luxurious environment to a tiny, two-room apartment in America, yet they were happier than they had ever been because they had escaped the Communists and the Nazis.

Despite all the tragedy he had experienced, my father appreciated his life and had a great attitude, which he passed on to me. I love to dance because he loved to dance. He loved comedies, and we were both crazy about Lucille Ball and Bob Hope. He didn't waste time watching tear-jerker shows; he didn't want to cry. I was always early for everything, while he was always late – he would even miss the beginning of his favourite television shows. He loved table tennis and was so good at it that he could have won tournaments. I was good too, but I could never beat him. When we were warming up for a game, as soon as I scored a point, I would claim that the game had already started so I could start off with an advantage. He also taught me how to play a special double solitaire game that I don't think anyone else in the world knows, and I am now teaching it to my grandson.

Some of my fondest memories are of the Sundays we spent at the Polish National Alliance (PNA) at Yorkville. Every Sunday from Memorial Day through Labor Day, we would have a picnic at the PNA, and my father would play pinochle and volleyball while I visited friends I had met during the summer camp that was offered by the PNA each year. Afterwards, we would stop at Dairy Queen on the way home for a special treat.

PREFACE

My father's attitude was that life is too short, so no time should be wasted in being miserable. He loved to laugh and make others laugh, and everybody loved him. He wanted to be cremated so people wouldn't remember him as just a body reposed in death, but as he was when he was alive: playing soccer, bowling and dancing.

This book was my father's dream – a dream that came true when it was first published in his native Poland in 2010. I am so happy that it is now being brought to the English-speaking world, and I know my father would be overjoyed as well.

Teresa Dambski Ponce De Leon
August 2023

Acknowledgements

AT THIS TIME, I would like to thank the publisher, Zbigniew Gluza, president of Fundacja Ośrodka KARTA (the KARTA Foundation), for publishing my dad's book in Poland. Also, thank you Agnieszka Dębska for being a very patient agent – all the contracts that you drew up and all the correspondence and emails that were sent from Poland to America trying to perfect Dad's story. I would like to thank my stepmother, Carole Dambski (recently deceased), for making my dad's last ten years the happiest of his life. Thank you to my wonderful husband, Jesse Ponce De Leon, for putting up with me and for his support and encouragement. Thank you to my stepdaughter, Genevieve Ponce De Leon, for our endless discussions about my dad. I am sure I repeated the same stories over and over, yet you would patiently listen and always smile at my enthusiasm and love for my dad. Lastly, I would like to thank my dear friend and editor, Chris Carson. We spent many hours also talking about my dad, and with her help and editing skills, I was able to compose this Preface.

Introduction

WARTIME RESISTANCE MOVEMENTS DEDICATED to fighting or undermining invaders are quickly created during times of war. People are compelled to act in ways they would never have imagined in peacetime, and this was certainly the case during the Second World War, when these movements occurred in every occupied country. One of particular note was the Polish Resistance, which started as early as September 1939, with the Armia Krajowa (Home Army) becoming the dominant movement once it had absorbed most of the other Polish partisan and Underground forces.

The Polish Underground State was built in complete secrecy during the joint occupation of Poland by Germany and the USSR. Nowhere in occupied Europe was there another such complex and well-working organization. Its most important task, alongside arranging Underground activity, was to provide unbroken functionality of the pre-war national institutions and make preparations for the taking back of power once the war was eventually won. The Home Army was subordinate in the military chain of command to the Commander-in-Chief of the Polish government-in-exile in London.

There have been various attempts at quantifying the Home Army's size, and debate continues, but according to Gregor Dallas in his book *1945: The War that Never Ended*, it numbered around 400,000 people in late 1943, making it the largest resistance organization in Europe. As noted in the *WIEM Encyklopedia*, in 1944 the Home Army included 10,000–11,000 officers, 7,500 officers-in-training and 88,000 non-commissioned officers. These included pre-war officers and NCOs, graduates of Underground courses and elite operatives, usually parachuted in from the West.

The basic organizational unit was a platoon of 35–50 people, with a skeleton version of 16–25 individuals that were not mobilized. In February 1944, the Home Army had 6,287 regular and 2,613 skeleton operational platoons. These were organized into various specialized units responsible for justice and religion, intelligence and counterintelligence, operations and training, logistics, communication, information and propaganda, finances and special operations. Its primary operations included the gathering of intelligence. According to Halik Kochanski in her book *The Eagle Unbowed: Poland and the Poles in the Second World War*, 48 per cent of all reports received by the British Secret Services from continental Europe between 1939 and 1945 came from Polish sources. Other activities included the freeing of prisoners and hostages, as well as military or sabotage operations. Many thousands of actions were undertaken, including the Zamość Rising of 1942–43, where the Home Army sabotaged German plans to expel Poles under *Generalplan Ost*. Another action of note was Operation *Belt* in 1943, a series of attacks on German border outposts. Operation *Tempest* in 1944 was a series of nationwide risings which aimed to seize control of cities and areas where German forces were preparing defences against the Red Army, so that Polish Underground civil authorities could take power before the arrival of Soviet forces. The largest and best-known of these battles was the Warsaw Uprising.

The Home Army also sabotaged German rail and road transport to the Eastern Front with the Soviet Union, with an eighth of all German transports destroyed or substantially delayed, according to Richard J Crampton in his book *Eastern Europe in the Twentieth Century*. In addition, they carried out dozens of attacks on senior Nazi commanders in Poland, such as Operation *Bürkl*, where Franz Bürkl, an SS-Oberscharführer, Gestapo officer and commandant of the Pawiak prison, was assassinated on 7 September 1943. Another example was the assassination of Franz Kutschera, an SS-Brigadeführer and police leader of the Warsaw district, on 1 February 1944.

Pertinent to the memoirs presented here, an activity that is perhaps broached less often is the fact that the Home Army also had to deal with Polish collaborators and traitors, on whom they carried out sentences that were handed down by the Underground State's courts. Collaboration and association with the enemy could take many forms, and not every type was immediately met with a death sentence. In some instances, people were visited and persuaded to act differently. The Home Army published a leaflet in 1943 which reminded people that 'Every Pole is obligated to help those in hiding. Those who refuse them aid will be punished on the basis of ... treason to the Polish Nation.' Indeed, the Home Army executed people who blackmailed Jews who were in hiding, or the Poles who aided them. An information bulletin from 2 September 1943 cites the example of Jan Grabiec, who was executed for blackmailing residents of villages that were sheltering Jews.

One chapter here concerns the Home Army responding to the mass murder of Poles by Ukrainians in Volhynia and Eastern Galicia. This genocide was committed by Ukrainian nationalists, with the active and frequent support of the local Ukrainian population, between February 1943 and February 1945. The victims of the murders were predominantly Poles, with much smaller numbers of Russians, Ukrainians, Jews, Armenians, Czechs and other nationalities who inhabited the area. The exact number of victims is not known, although historians estimate that between 50,000 and 100,000 Poles were killed. In return, it is believed that 2,000–3,000 Ukrainians were killed by Poles in retaliation.

The history of Polish–Ukrainian friction runs deep. Centuries earlier, the eastern territories of the multinational First Polish Republic had been inhabited predominantly by

INTRODUCTION

Poles, Lithuanians, Belarusians, Ukrainians, Jews and Tatars. The Polish population lived mainly – although not exclusively – in the larger cities and constituted the local elite, while the Ukrainian population predominantly made up the labour force in the large landed estates, where serfdom and the peasant's ties to the land were common. Consequently, there were numerous revolts by the Ukrainian population and Cossacks against Polish magnates and landowners. Later, in the years 1918–20, Ukrainians had also tried to create their own state but were ultimately unsuccessful, with the eastern lands eventually becoming part of the Soviet Union, and the western lands a part of the reborn Republic of Poland. The interwar period was a time of national rebirth in the Second Polish Republic, following 123 years of non-existence on the map of Europe as a result of its partition by Austria, Russia and Prussia. Unfortunately for the Ukrainians, in Poland it was also the time of the implementation of a new state policy concerning nationality that discriminated against them. During this time, 5 million Polish citizens identified themselves as having Ukrainian nationality, and relations between them and Poles were marked by numerous tensions following efforts at Polonization and the revindication of Orthodox churches.

Move forward a few years, and by 1942, the ruthless conduct of the occupying Germans had led to the spontaneous development of Ukrainian partisan movements, with the Ukrainian Insurgent Army (UPA) and the Organization of Ukrainian Nationalists (OUN) being most notable. The defeat of Germany at Stalingrad in February 1943 and the prospect of the Red Army entering eastern Poland caused Polish citizens of Ukrainian nationality to consider their country's independence again. The OUN feared a repetition of what happened after the First World War, when the vacuum had been filled by the Poles. The gates of hell were opened: Polish houses, churches and other buildings were burned. In order to shock the Poles, the Ukrainians killed them as brutally and gruesomely as possible. Children were impaled on fence stakes, women's bellies were cut open, babies were thrown into burning houses, heads were cut off, eyes gouged out, teeth broken, tongues ripped out through holes in the throat, as well as rape, burning, chopping with axes. They were so cruel, that sometimes even Germans ended up protecting Poles. Polish self-defence units began to form immediately, although they were few in number, poorly armed and their activity was limited to patrolling an area and warning of an upcoming attack. There was reaction to the assaults, as well as revenge attacks by the Home Army. At the beginning of January 1944, Operation *Tempest* was started in an effort to seize control of German-occupied cities and areas ahead of the advancing Soviet Red Army. A number of combat operations against UPA units were also conducted.

By the war's end, Dąmbski was one of approximately 2 million Poles who found themselves in Germany, the overwhelming majority having been forced labourers, prisoners of war and captives in various German camps. Many of these people decided not to return to Communist Poland, and so a new life had to be organized. The Allies were conscious that the presence of these people would be a future problem that had to be dealt with in advance. Already by 1943, the so-called Outline Plan for Refugees and Displaced Persons was drawn up in order to address this. As a result, a new category of person was defined: the so-called 'displaced person', or DP.

As already noted, Stefan Dąmbski served in a US Guard Company after he had reached the Western occupation zone in July 1945, just weeks after Germany's surrender on 7 May. The displaced persons' reluctance to return to Poland was intensified by the attitude of the Polish government in London, who believed their return could be seen as a form of legitimization of the new authorities in Warsaw that were totally subordinate to the Soviets. A means of remaining in the West was offered by service in the Labor Service Companies of the American Army, which were first set up during the war. In September 1944, Colonel Janusz Ilinski, on behalf of the Polish military authorities in London, signed an agreement in Versailles with the American command in Europe for the creation of Polish Labour Service units, first deployed in France and then in Germany to perform auxiliary technical work and guard duty.

The units continued until the late 1970s, becoming an obscure phenomenon of the Cold War. Over their lifetime thousands of citizens of countries occupied by the Soviet Union joined them. Initially, Poles constituted the largest group. Many Polish volunteers and exiled political leaders hoped that these new formations would become the beginnings of a 'Polish Legion', to be used during the anticipated upcoming conflict with the Soviets. However, the guard companies ultimately became auxiliary and paramilitary organizations used for security, technical and transport duties.

In the transition to a peacetime footing, the US and its allies needed thousands of people to protect military installations, warehouses, prison camps, civilian representatives and army officers. There was an urgent need for additional manpower to assist the US Military Police in fighting the crime that plagued the American occupation zone. Coming with a wealth of wartime experience, the Polish guards could easily fill this role. At their peak, the number of guards reached 40,000 and included over 21,000 Poles. They wore American uniforms, and emphasized their nationality not only with their language, but also with a cap badge showing a crowned eagle, and a shoulder patch emblazoned with the word POLAND. They were equipped with weapons in order to help keep order in post-war Germany.

Marek Sobieralski
February 2023

1

Entry

I REALIZE THESE MEMORIES will probably never appear on any bookstore shelves. So many years have passed since I left my homeland and started my wanderings in various foreign countries, unable to return to the Poland for whose freedom I once fought.

I survived the war, but of the first 300 boys who were with me in 1942, only a few dozen are alive today. Three died on free American soil; the rest fell on the 'field of glory', many by my side. Only two of those who were killed were over 20 years of age.

Time passes quickly, and I don't have much time left. Every few years, I meet veterans from the Home Army in Chicago. We talk of old times in whispers. […] The partisan experiences are not spoken about. I don't want to believe that such a large part of Polish history from the Second World War can be lost forever. So much Polish blood was spilled, and for what? These young people, who died next to me every day, had no families, had no surnames – you forgot about them the next day. 'You today, and me tomorrow,' as we said back then. […]

My codename during the war was 'Żbik I' (Wildcat I). I held the position of squad leader, and within four years of service, I reached the rank of master corporal. I belonged to two units of the Home Army: in the Underground, I belonged to the 'Józef'* Unit of the Second Rzeszów Outpost, whose headquarters were in Nieborów; after Operation *Burza* (*Tempest*), I was transferred to 'D14' Company, that is, the Fourteenth Jazłowiec Lancers Regiment of the Home Army, which came within the grouping of the Lwów 'Warta' district.

I was decorated with the Cross of Valour, which I valued very much, mainly because this was awarded to only four boys from our section. You didn't hear about the *Virtuti Militari* in the Fourteenth.

I have a 'Statement of Verification' No. L.dz. 279/47, issued by the Independent Department of Liquidation, for matters relating to Home Army soldiers on the territory of the American occupation zone in Germany, signed by the head of the department, Major Kazimierz Piotrowski.

I was drawn into the Home Army by a good pre-war friend [Stanisław Pałac]; he was older than me and held the rank of second lieutenant in the Underground. He did not belong

---

* 'Józef' was Mieczysław Chendyński (1901–54), from the beginning of 1941 deputy and then commander of the Hyżne Outpost, and from May 1944 deputy commander of the Rzeszów-South Home Army sub-district. He was commander of units of the Eleventh Grouping of Rzeszow-East.

to the Fourteenth, which came into my Rzeszów territories much later, but to the 'Józef' Second Outpost. His codename was 'Stach' (Stan). He was my direct commander and 'contact'. I took the oath in front of him in a little country cottage with a candle lit on the Bible.

It was only two weeks after I had been sworn in that I met our boys from the Underground for the first time. I was somewhat disappointed. They didn't carry weapons. They did not have any training. Their task was just carrying messages. That's where I started too.

After joining the ranks of the Home Army, I expected more action and excitement; I dreamed of fame. But here, for the first three months, nothing happened. Every two days, I set off with reports that I'd picked up from under one stone, only to carry them and put under another rock that was 15 kilometres away. […]

Back then, I lived in the countryside with my brother and aunt, and I started dreaming about leaving the house and moving to be with the partisans. I knew difficult conditions awaited me in the forests, but I also felt I would have a varied life there, filled with the powerful excitement I'd always sought. Making the decision was easy, but getting in there was another matter. I'd heard about 'Józef', but I had no access to him, and didn't know where to find him. Help came my way entirely by accident.

At that time, I had a friend called Jurek – a great all-round guy. It was interesting that while he was not in the Home

Army, he somehow always chose Home Army guys for buddies. And then a bomb goes off!

One afternoon, 'Stach' comes to me and says that I should be careful what I say to Jurek because it turned out that he saw the Gestapo regularly every week. 'Stach' asked me to see Jurek just as before, until the boys arrived from the unit that would carry out his liquidation.

I immediately saw a great opportunity. I told 'Stach' that I had a Polish carbine hidden under my bed and asked him to let me finish Jurek off. I said I would suggest to him that we went deer-hunting, an activity which I secretly did in any case, and the matter would be settled. At first 'Stach' didn't want to hear about it; he explained that I didn't have the experience, that Jurek would sense something, that it could be a trap, that he was very shrewd. After an hour of persuasion, he agreed to everything, though reluctantly.

After 'Stach' had left, I took a deep breath. […] Somehow, it never occurred to me that in a few hours I was going to shoot a man, that I had to kill not only a human being but also my friend, with whom I had drunk many bottles of moonshine. I saw this as something absolutely normal, that had to be done to fulfil one's ordinary patriotic duty. The fact that I had volunteered my services was unimportant.

The day after my conversation with 'Stach', Jurek came over. My aunt went to the rectory. We were alone in the house. Jurek, happy as always, told me the news of the past two days.

ENTRY

I took a bottle out of the cupboard, poured some into glasses, and we hit the gas.

After he was nicely oiled, I started casually to admit gently, as if drunk, how I love hunting very much and that I even have a carbine hidden at home, and if he wanted, I would gladly take him for some deer tonight. […] He immediately agreed. He looked at my carbine admiringly and praised its good condition – as if it had just come out of the factory. We drank one for the road, I put the carbine under my cape and we walked onto the first forest path less than half an hour later.

I walked first, my gun was loaded. Then I remembered 'Stach's' last words to me: 'And don't forget to read him the sentence, let him know what he's dying for!'

I also began to remember the words of the judgment: 'On behalf of the Government of the Republic of Poland, and on behalf of the Command of the Home Army ...' Nonsense, I thought, what use is that sentence to him right now?

We passed the second forest clearing. I knew every corner and every tree here. I turned quickly. Jurek was walking briskly, smiling. I didn't have to aim from such close range. I shot instantly, holding my carbine at the ready. Jurek took one more step forward; the smile died on his lips and, without a word, he fell to the ground like a log.

2

Partisan

TWO WEEKS LATER I was already with the partisans. 'Stach' arranged everything. I was introduced to 'Józef' himself. A brief report on me, only superlatives. I was in seventh heaven. I joined Józek [Zawory] 'Czarny's' platoon. A magnificent guy: cold, composed, taciturn – my type of partisan. I tried to imitate him. I felt he liked me.

Our platoon now had a lot of intense training in the depths of the Rzeszów forests, close to Nieborów. I learned to shoot with a pistol. For now, I'm using a borrowed gun because I only brought the carbine with me, which was – as I found out later – entirely out of fashion here. Ammunition was doled out like medicine, so it could only be allowed in basic training. Everyone dreamed of a submachine gun. […] There were not many examples of this type of weapon; they were used on patrols or lent to colleagues undertaking more extensive missions.

As for me, I armed myself sooner than I expected. […]

I was sitting quietly on surveillance at the edge of the forest along with my carbine, when 'Czarny' (Black) came to relieve me. And suddenly, a boy from the village ran up.

'Gentlemen!' he calls out breathlessly. 'Germans are at the grange in Hyżne and have arrested one of your boys!'

It is less than a kilometre to the farm. Józek and I run there at full speed. Indeed, there's a lad from our unit, we recognize him immediately. It is Mietek 'Szaj'. He is already sitting in the Mercedes. He has no weapon. The Germans don't know who they have, they arrested him because they found meat in his possession, and that alone is enough to make sure he is not long for this world.

Looking out from behind the wall of the building, we evaluate the situation. Two Germans in uniform, one man in civilian clothes and a driver at the wheel. The civilian is standing by the car and is already saying goodbye to the grange manager. There's nothing to wait for.

One German is sitting dangerously close to Mietek. I point him out with my finger to 'Czarny'. He understands: too far away for the automatic. I take aim at him with my rifle. I aim for the head so that it's further from Mietek. 'Count,' I tell 'Czarny'. I hear: 'One, two, three …' We pull our triggers simultaneously. Both soldiers fall to the ground. The civilian dives into the open car.

We run up closer, sheltered by the trees in the courtyard. 'Hands up!' I shout in German. Both the driver and the civilian stand up from the floor of the car and raise their hands. The grange manager is standing near the bonnet of the Mercedes

16

as if petrified. Mietek is as pale as a wall – but whole – and jumps out of the back seat. We load two dead bodies into the car and take the civilian with us. The driver is a Pole – we order him to take us down a dirt road to the forest.

On the way, we check the civilian's ID. Not good: he's an important figure. To this day, I remember his name – Pillman, Kreislandwirt [head of the Department of Agriculture], the most important person in Rzeszów after the city mayor. The entire population of the province knew him. He set 'quotas', and he allocated *Bezugsscheins* [coupons]. We quickly understand that because of him, the Germans could pacify the whole of Hyżne. Every tenth Pole in this village will be shot.

Having reached the edge of the forest, we leave the car and go to 'Józef' for orders. We find him by the fire. We give a detailed report. Mietek gets it for his idiotic walk through the centre of the farm, where the German car was standing. He explains that it did not occur to him that the Germans would look into the sack he was carrying. But it happened.

'Józef' made a decision. Take the car back to the village with the driver. Give him clear instructions. After returning to Rzeszów he should convey to his superiors that Pillman is safe and well, and being held captive by partisans. As long as no hair on a Pole's head is harmed over the next six months we will release a healthy Pillman after this time.

We carry out the plan straight away. Two lads take the driver and the car to the village, from where they let him go free after giving him his instructions. One of my new friends,

'Majeranek' (Marjoram) [Kazimierz Stankiewicz], now joins Pillman and me, walking into the depths of the Hyżneński gorge. 'Majeranek' has a shovel over his shoulder, and Pillman walks half-dead with fear, gibbering incomprehensible words under his breath. [...] We get to the forest. From under my belt I take a pistol which a few hours earlier had belonged to Pillman, and shoot him in the back of the head from a distance of five centimetres. A great weapon, it sits in the hand beautifully – I think – looking at the German lying on the ground like a sack of sand. One more shot, the so-called security shot, then 'Majeranek' and I take turns working with the shovel.

The Germans never found out what happened to Pillman. Apparently they waited the half-year, as per the instructions, and then it was too late to pacify the village.

Months went by. Winter passed, and the year 1943 had begun. That winter was the first one I spent in the 'forest'. I put the last word in quotation marks because I spent most nights in the villages, in the homes of the lads from the Underground. It was much riskier for them than for me. Their whole families lived in constant fear of arrest or death for hiding partisans.

[...] During my first year with the partisans, about thirty of my best colleagues died. [...] We had connections in the Gestapo and the Polish uniformed police. In most instances, we were warned by these gentlemen of upcoming round-ups to Germany or of exposures. These people were worth their weight in gold to us. There weren't many of them. [...] One such precious connection was none other than the commander of the Polish uniformed police in Tyczyn, a small town located 8 kilometres south-east of Rzeszów.

We had a piece of bad luck when I was sent along with 'Wilk' (Wolf) [Jan Gąsior] and 'Majeranek' on an assignment to Rzeszów. We stopped for breakfast in the only open restaurant in the town, where we ordered buttered bread rolls, which we started eating eagerly while sipping coffee. Suddenly the door opens, and three policemen in the navy-blue uniform of the Polish police enter. One of them (whom we didn't know) was the commander himself, who – seeing strange faces – decided to ask us for documents.

Seeing that one of the police officers had put his hand on his handgun, we all simultaneously grabbed our guns from under our belts. 'Majeranek' floors the commander with one shot, while 'Wilk' and I hit the deck and open fire on the remaining two. The entire episode lasted no more than five seconds.

It was two weeks later, after returning to my unit, that I found out that one of the police officers who was killed worked for the Home Army. […]

To perform a liquidation 'cleanly' you had to have not only the right preparation, but also skill and weapons. It was also important always to go with the same guys. As most of the work did not require more than three partisans, we formed groups that always operated together. As a result, the three knew each other very well, trusted each other absolutely, and – in the event of a sudden, alarming situation – knew without saying what to do. The weapons had to be first-class and reliable too. […]

During my second year with the partisans, as far as work in the city was concerned, my typical weapon was a standard 9 mm. My favourite was a German semi-automatic pistol, a very accurate gun, and almost perfectly reliable if kept clean. Contrary to popular belief, revolvers, in various sizes and calibres, were very impractical. Although they never jammed, because, in the event of a misfire, the pressure on the trigger moved the drum round one position – so the weapon remained armed – they had two significant drawbacks. The first was that you had extremely limited firepower. It was often the case that seemingly easy tasks resulted in complications, as a result of which a greater number of shots was needed. You could only fire six from the revolver – and then what? Maybe 'hands up'? Unlike the automatic pistol, where you simply had to put in a new magazine after firing nine rounds, the revolver required much longer to change the used shells for fresh cartridges. Secondly, it was inaccurate because it had no safety catch, and it was necessary to pull the trigger very hard when firing, which often caused the barrel to wobble, resulting in inaccuracy when firing.

I have always attached great importance to the calibre of a gun. […] Speed is the most crucial thing for surprise. Nerves also play a significant role. As far as the small calibre of a pistol is concerned, a badly shot opponent can sometimes remain conscious for a long time. If he has his own revolver or a pistol in his pocket – he is still capable of defending himself, often with disastrous results.

A great gun was the Polish Vis, produced in pre-war Radom, although unfortunately, it was very difficult for us to obtain. Other good 9 mm guns were: the Spanish Lama, German P38, Russian TT and Mauser. We also got American Colt 45s from British air drops. We converted them to our calibre; they were 12 mm. With a good gun, a person hit in the leg would die from blood loss within half an hour. However, these were impractical as we couldn't get the ammunition at all, so after firing the one pack of cartridges that came with the gun, it could be thrown into the garbage.

I usually went on missions in the villages fully armed, so as well as the pistol, I also took a machine gun. During the German occupation I had a German one; during the Soviet occupation a Russian one. The English Stens were nice because they didn't jam, but they had a slow rate of fire and were inaccurate. The best were Russian Pepeszkas,* which could be used with either 72-round drums or 32-round magazines. These magazines were 100 per cent certain. Defensive grenades were only used in larger actions. We did

---

* The PPSz-41, or 'Pistolet-pulemyot Sudayeva' is a Soviet submachine gun, developed as a low-cost personal defence weapon for reconnaissance units, vehicle crews and support service personnel. It was commonly known in Poland as a 'Pepeszka'. Despite its crudeness, it has been described as functional, practical, controllable and reliable.

not take them on lighter duties so as to not burden ourselves unnecessarily. During my own training, the emphasis was on drawing my gun quickly and taking a lightning-fast shot. […]

In the summer of 1943, I reported – voluntarily, of course – for a four-week stay in Rzeszów in order to rob the Germans of pistols. I had quarters arranged, a small room in an attic on Grunwaldzka Street. On market day, I arrive in town on a peasant's cart, the gun hidden in the straw. A lad from the local Underground is waiting for me. After exchanging passwords, he guides me to my quarters, raises a hand in farewell, and that's all I see of him.

For the first week, I carefully observe two German nightclubs. I watch the Krauts as they go to the park with some girls. During the day, I find a hollow in an old lime tree that was growing just two steps away from a park bench. I put my pistol there and will get to work on the next Monday. I start at around nine in the evening. Knowing about the curfew, the Germans leave the club a bit earlier to take care of their love urges with the ladies. And here I am, waiting. I have good, well-forged papers on me, so I sit calmly on the bench.

An enamoured couple passes me, and instead of looking at the girl's legs, I cut to the gun in the Kraut's holster. I'm not even interested in a Walther 7.65 – it has to be a 9 mm. I let the three couples pass before the first victim appeared on the horizon in the form of a Wehrmacht officer with a large pistol at his side. I quickly reach into the hollow and pull out my gun; I poke it under the officer's ribs and politely ask for his gun. After giving the loving couple instructions on how they should behave after my departure, I put the pistols under my belt and briskly walk back to the hiding place.

I returned unarmed to the same park the following evening for orientation. I saw lots of Krauts ID-ing passers-by. I waited a whole week and did a similar job in another Rzeszów park, after which I switched to the banks of the river Wisłok. There I took another two new pistols and decided to call it a day. I sensed it was just a matter of time before they uncover me. If I'm to die, it should be by chance and not by stupidity.

It's market day on Monday, and I meet a farmer friend from Dylągówka. He drives me to the village without a clue that I am carrying as many as four captured pistols, plus my own, in the small bag I have with me.

The occupation was doing its thing, so more and more people took refuge with us. It was mostly young lads who came, completely 'exposed', without families, without homes. They came for a variety of reasons. Some for patriotic con-siderations, others because they were threatened with arrest or deportation to work in Germany. It is true to say that the volunteers were mainly from the first category, but that didn't make them heroes yet. [...]

The partisans gave the lads a chance – albeit minimal – of surviving the war, giving a lad a certain kind of care. High command was concerned for him: what he would eat for dinner, where he would sleep, and what he was doing ... He felt needed here. And he was indeed needed because without these boys, the Home Army would not be able to exist, nor could it carry out major actions. [...] I don't deny that partisan life was convenient for me and people like me. I didn't have to go to school, which I hadn't enjoyed during my young years, I didn't have to undertake physical work, I didn't have any family obligations, and I didn't have to worry about what I would put in the pot tomorrow. I hated a monotonous life, and I had variety and emotions of many kinds with the partisans.

Individual liquidations were mostly carried out on a voluntary basis. Our unit, with 'Józef' and later with 'Draża',* did not use more than ten or at most fifteen lads for a mission. [...] They were people who were always prepared for any job and were well known to the command, having made a name for themselves so that they were simply chosen routinely, depending on their qualifications.

What did a lad have to have inside himself in order to be really good at these tasks? What was needed was training, good physical condition, and – the main thing – cold blood, composure. Achieving the latter was not all that easy. Everyone had to work on that individually. [...] You need to eliminate fear. I think this is only possible in young people under the

---

* Dragan M. Sotirović, aka 'Draża', 'Michał', 'X' (1913–87) – captain of the Yugoslav Army, a Serb. After establishing contact with the Home Army, he became deputy commander of forest units of the Fourteenth Cavalry Regiment. Arrested by the NKVD on 31 July 1944, he escaped from prison and made his way beyond the San River to the Rzeszów region to branches of 'Warta'. He commanded the D14 Company. In the summer of 1945, he left for France, became a French citizen and changed his name to Jacques Roman.

age of 20 [...]. The older a man is, the more he knows, and the more he wants to live. [...]

During the days, I worked on myself. I was running away from reality. I lived an endless imagination, persuaded myself that I wouldn't survive this war, and even if I did get through it by some miracle, that I wouldn't have a happy future ahead, so my death was the only answer. Living with this premise for months, I finally believed it. And this is what made me so good.

At one time, I was the pride of the entire unit. Since it made no difference to me if I lived, I did not care at all if others lived. I shot at people like at a target during training, without any emotion. I liked to see the terrified faces before the liquidation, and I liked to watch the blood gushing from the head wound.

My dreams had come true; I was unscrupulous ... I was worse than the vilest animal, and at the very bottom of the human swamp. And yet I was a typical Home Army soldier. I was a hero on whose chest was pinned the Cross of Valour after the war, one of four issued for the entire Fourteenth Unit.

3

Work

IT'S NOW THE AUTUMN of 1943. Germany is clearly withdrawing from the Eastern Front more and more. […] My hands are now full due to work. The Home Army got seriously to work at getting even with all the *Volksdeutsche*.

I'm on liquidations all the time. I return to my unit, have one day of rest, and go into the field again. […] I mostly go with 'Majeranek' and 'Wilk'. […]

The liquidation of Mr Baran in Rzeszów. Although he had a pure Polish surname, he was a *Volksdeutsche*. He sent many a Pole to concentration camps, and for that, quite reasonably, he was given the death penalty. Two of us go to Rzeszów, 'Majeranek' and me. We march determinedly all night […] we get to Rzeszów early in the morning. A local contact is already waiting for us at 3 Maja Street. We go to the building where Mr Baran lives and wait for about half an hour. At precisely eight in the morning, Mr Baran leaves and heads towards the Gestapo building. Our local contact, who was with us to aid identification, says only one word, 'Him,' and goes away in the opposite direction.

'Majeranek' now goes to the other side of the street as 'insurance', and I rush after Baran. I get to within a stride's distance behind him, calmly take out my pistol, put it almost right up to his head and pull the trigger ... And nothing happens ... I just hear a gentle 'click'! Damn, I think, I got a misfire. I try to reload the pistol, and must have done it too hurriedly, as the next bullet gets stuck endways in the breechblock.

Mr Baran isn't the dunderhead he looks like. He has turned, assessed the situation immediately, and – not waiting for anything – takes his gun from his pocket. [...] I do a quick 180-degree turn and start hurtling away at a speed many Olympians would envy.

I don't think I've run more than ten steps before Mr Baran opens fire behind me. Total Sodom and Gomorrah on the streets. I run in a zigzag, desperately trying to stay alive. 'Majeranek' tears down the other side of the street. It's full of people here. They run through open gates or fall scared onto the ground, and Mr Baran thinks nothing of it; he releases a whole magazine towards me.

Maybe this story would have ended tragically if it was not for a chance event that helped me. At that moment, some high-ranking German officer drove into the street in a carriage. He saw Mr Baran, in civilian clothes, firing indiscriminately in the street. Since he did not know him, he mistook him for a partisan who was trying to liquidate someone. Not pausing to think, he pulled his automatic from its holster, took aim at Mr Baran, and fired half a magazine into him.

When I eventually got to the corner of the street, I looked back and had to rub my eyes because I thought I couldn't see clearly. Mr Baran was lying stretched out in the road, and standing over him was the heroic Nazi, gun in hand.

'Majeranek' and I return to our unit. 'Józef' isn't there, so we report to Lieutenant 'Rysio' [Tadeusz Wrażeń]. We give a short report on a successful liquidation. We don't go into details. The sentence was carried out, exactly how was nobody's business.

*

APPROXIMATELY 30 KILOMETRES SOUTH of Rzeszów was a small village called Harta. The local population mainly consisted of smallholders whose main concern was feeding their families. They did not get involved with politics; they went to church every Sunday and waited for a better tomorrow. A beautiful girl was born and raised in this village, Jadzia Pierożanka. She'd completed seventh grade at school, and compared to others in the rural areas had a so-called future ahead of her.

She had light blonde hair, blue eyes and a figure that was out of this world. After the death of her father, who died in a sawmill accident, she lived with her mother and her younger sister. It was pretty inevitable that lads not only from Harta, but also from all nearby villages would be interested in beautiful Jadzia.

Jadzia liked to have a good time, so she attended all the local dances and weddings, which did not always end happily. It happened more than once that one of Jadzia's weaker suitors would return home with a broken head, which a stronger rival had smashed with a whippletree. Still, Jadzia liked specific men. One of them was Bronek Pieniowski. […]

He liked to sing, and that impressed Jadzia the most. She completely lost her head for Bronek when at a friend's wedding, surrounded as always by a swarm of admirers, she saw with her own eyes how Bronek, offended by the lack of space for himself at the side of his beloved, rose from his chair and, standing in front of the orchestra, intoned with a strong, clear voice: 'Give way, you grandads, give way, you suckers, because damn it I'll drive you away. You all had your dances, I did not disturb you, so now I'll throwing you out of the way!' Having finished, he walked ceremoniously over to the corner of the room, from which he produced a well-kept horse-bar, shod with iron on each side. The sight of the bar gave everyone to understand that the fun was over and that the next dance would take place during the traditional re-party the next day. The hall was empty within a minute; those who had not made it to the door, escaped through windows.

A great romance began between Bronek and beautiful Jadzia. […] However, Bronek believed that man does not live by love alone. […] the marriage should be postponed while the Fatherland had urgent need of him because, after all, wars cannot be rescheduled. Jadzia's pleas, tears and tempting smiles did not help. […] Bronek made a decision. He loved his girlfriend and confessed everything to her. He said he would join the partisans' ranks to fight for the Fatherland.

Bronek Pieniowski was assigned to our unit in the autumn of 1943. I liked him very much for his honesty and openness; I taught him partisan tricks when time allowed. […] He told me everything about Jadzia. I congratulated him on this love. Meanwhile, Jadzia was overwhelmed by despair after Bronek's departure. She no longer saw a purpose to her life. […]

She began to seek revenge on her fiancé. […] She went to the local Gestapo and sang. She told them that her Bronek had joined the partisans, that he had a gun … The Gestapo sent a punishment squad which liquidated Bronek's entire family. His mother, father, two brothers and a sister, and even an uncle who was staying overnight with Bronek's parents, were shot during the raid.

Two weeks after the tragedy, Jadzia's fate is sealed. I leave the quarters before sunrise and have an automatic under my coat. I drop in on 'Majeranek' on the way. We are going to Harta. Walking all day, we get there at around six in the evening. I remember today how I thought about Bronek on the way. The lad didn't know it was me doing this job.

There, we find a lad from the local Underground. It's already dark. He takes us to Jadzia's house and leaves. We are by the windows. I see three silhouettes. She's home – I think. We knock and, not waiting for an answer, enter the room through the open door. I recognize Jadzia straight away. I heard so much about her from Bronek. What a beautiful girl! Her long hair and those big blue eyes … She sees us, and I notice that she turns as white as paper.

'Jadzia Pierożanka?' I ask, looking straight into her eyes.

'Yes, that's me […].'

I hear her voice trembling, trying to keep her composure to the end. Her little sister is standing petrified, her mother faints and falls to the ground. I read the judgment. 'You have been sentenced to death for treason against the Polish state; the sentence will be carried out immediately. I give you ten minutes to pray and say goodbye to your family.'

My calm voice is doing its work, and tears as big as peas appear in Jadzia's eyes. The sister lunges at her with a spasmodic cry around her neck, and I see how they pick up the fainting mother and lay her on a bed. I watch as Jadzia makes the sign of the cross on her chest, and I hear her whisper a prayer. A few minutes pass this way. Eventually, I take Jadzia's hand and head towards the door. I pass 'Majeranek' standing inert at the door. I can see his eyes are wet. A few more steps to the barn. I stand Jadzia, half-conscious with fear, beside it, facing me; I take one step back and raise the automatic. I aim straight for her head. It's a moonlit night, I can see this beautiful creature in front of me, and at the last moment, I feel some kind of regret.

WORK

I lower the barrel and pull the trigger at the same time. Anywhere but in the head, I think– how will she look in the coffin? A long burst ... and it's all over! Jadzia Pierożanka ceases to exist ... why? That was a question that haunted me for weeks.

*

AT THE BEGINNING OF 1944, the defeat of the Germans was becoming more and more visible. We saw reinforcements heading east much less frequently. In the villages around Rzeszów, one could notice a certain kind of easing of pressure. The previously endless round-ups had stopped, and Gestapo and gendarmerie activities were slowly coming to an end. There was also a certain stagnation in liquidations. There was a period of three weeks where I didn't undertake any missions, nor did I shoot one person. There was simply no one to shoot. We dealt with the *Volksdeutsche* and their supporters. Those who remained alive – and believe me, there were just a handful – either escaped deep into Germany or hid in larger cities after changing their names. [...]

Our sabotage unit at the 'Józef' Second Outpost had almost doubled in size. Now, the boys (I write boys because, apart from the officers, I don't remember anybody being over 20 years of age) who had spent the entire period of occupation with the partisans no longer feared violence against their families because the Germans had a mass of troubles of their own, trying to maintain the front.

These boys brought mostly ancient weapons with them, many of which were from pre-war times. You would see old Mausers, and more than one greeted us with a small 6 mm. As most of them had never fired the weapons they brought, they underwent intense training in the forest clearings. In addition to shooting practice, they did basic military drills, went on surveillance and short patrols …

*

At this time, Lieutenant 'Ryś' was looking for volunteers for so-called 'women's work'. I offered my services immediately and urged 'Majeranek' and 'Wilk' to accompany me. 'Women's work' wasn't liquidation work, only a gentle reckoning with those women who liked to play with the Germans for money or their own pleasure. […] After all, these young ladies knew every neighbour in the village; they knew everything about who kept in touch with whom, where they went … I'm convinced that many unexplained arrests by Germans could be attributed to these young ladies.

As a definitive betrayal could not be proven against any of these girls, the Home Army command decided not to liquidate them, but just to give them a warning for the future in the form of corporal punishment. The imposition of such a penalty consisted of the complete shaving of their heads, or rather a haircut, plus twenty-five lashes on their bare bottoms. My trio was not the first to be sent out on such a job; a year earlier, other lads attended to it. If the first lesson didn't help a specific woman, the next was more severe, in that her hair – which would have somewhat grown back in the meantime – was not only cut again, but also smeared with a particular tar that caused chronic hair loss and complete baldness for a while. […]

The three of us worked on one village in the course of an evening. The first step was to contact a local guide. He would either already have a list ready, or would lead us to the village administrator and – if he worked with the Underground – would give us prepared names and house numbers on a piece of paper. The work was started early in the evening, in order to finish before midnight, after which time access to the houses would be very difficult. We were always in the company of a local guide who – although he didn't actually enter the home himself – was essential, as he knew all the thoroughfares and houses.

We worked like a well-coordinated sports team. 'Wilk' held the girl, I cut her hair to the skin with hairdressing scissors (I had experience of this because I once sheared sheep in an agricultural school), and 'Majeranek' finished off by smacking the already shorn victim with a rubber truncheon on her bare bottom. […]

[During one of the actions] we came to a cottage as usual; we took our positions at the rear and front doors, then introduced ourselves politely through the window, reporting the purpose of our visit. But in this case the dad had some nervous disorder and started shouting: 'You, motherfuckers, you will look at my Magda over my dead body!'

'Majeranek' smashed the window and climbed inside. And here, the dad swung an axe. He nearly chopped the lad's legs off. We got serious straight away, grabbed our pistols and fired! After hearing the lamentations of the women that arose in the house, it was easy to guess that dad didn't exist any more. We left without finishing the job. Magda had already received a far greater punishment than she was due.

*

YOU MIGHT GET THE impression that there was no discipline with us in the Home Army, that you could kill innocent people that were not the mission objective. It wasn't like that. We had to submit to special military laws which, if broken, would meant that we would face various disciplinary penalties. Just like in the regular army: you could receive criminal records, or even field courts martial.

One of the most serious offences was, of course, betrayal of the Polish state – squealing to the Gestapo or occupation authorities about any type of partisan or Underground secret. It was the same for civilians: vodka or no vodka, you had to keep your mouth shut. There were no excuses after something like that! You could not allow yourself to get arrested and then, under any kind of torture, save your own life by informing on your friends. A field court under the direction of the unit commander would pronounce judgment – sometimes even without the participation of the guilty party, who after the hearing was asked to turn to face 'that large tree'. There was no need for an execution squad, there was no need for a black blindfold or similar fuss. A simple shot to the back of the head from a former colleague was enough.

When you were ordered by the command to undertake a task, it was imperative that you carried it out. If we had, for example, given way to that girl's father, everyone would have slammed their doors in our face, and we wouldn't have been able to do this type of work. I feel for this father's situation, I realize that I might have done the same in his place, but I couldn't let the angry father chop off 'Majeranek's' leg. The order we were given might be questionable here, but its execution cannot be faulted.

At around eight in the morning, platoon leader 'Orzeł' (Eagle) came to our headquarters with an order for me. I was assigned to a patrol heading towards Tyczyna. The purpose of the patrol was to stay close to the main Rzeszów highway and seize single goods vehicles travelling with provisions in the direction of Rzeszów. Apart from 'Orzeł' and me, 'Majeranek' plus nine other boys went on this mission.

We march out punctually at nine, and after half an hour, we see the Rzeszów highway. In addition to our pistols, we each have machine guns and spare magazines. After three hours of steady walking, we enter Borek Stary, where instead of the expected goods vehicles, we see something entirely different. Two German tanks are a few metres from the road, but without crews and with their hatches open. We are surprised to see them and don't really know what to do with these prizes. Before we can decide, the crew jump out from the hut opposite – they must have noticed our group through the window and now want to jump back into their tanks.

We don't have time for a debate. We assess the situation on the spot. If the Germans get into their tanks, they will destroy us with their cannons. We throw ourselves into the ditch by the road and open fire with our automatics. There are eight of them in all. Three of them fall after our first volley; the rest, seeing that they cannot get into their tanks, throw themselves to the ground and open fire on us with their side arms.

The firefight is fierce. Two of our guys on the left side break away from us and come down on the Krauts from the side. I am first from the right in the ditch, 'Majeranek' is lying next to me. We now hear those two lads open fire from the side; we hear the screams of the dying Germans. I shoot straight ahead, in short bursts, trying to find the target. I'm already using my second 32-round magazine. Someone else was shooting at us. I thought it was the last two Germans. Suddenly I hear 'Majeranek' shout: 'Stefan, watch out!'

I look to the right. One of the surviving Germans has come at us from our right flank and got into our ditch. I can see his black uniform clearly, less than 10 metres away from me. As I am lying the first on the right, 'Majeranek', who had noticed him, couldn't shoot because he was afraid he might hit me by mistake. At that moment, the German opens fire straight at me.

I see the flash from him firing almost right in my eyes; I can literally hear the slide. Completely instinctively, I lower my machine gun from its previous position. I pull the trigger, although the barrel is not yet aligned with the target. At last, the moment when my bullets hit Kraut's head. I can see how his face turns into one red mass. Those were the final shots of the action. The other German had already died at the hands of my colleagues. Now silence ensues. I get up slowly and dust myself off.

I look to the left. I can see now that 'Majeranek' is lying motionless on his back. I can see his open eyes; I see the blood trickling down from the wound in his head. I know right away that he is dead, you don't survive an injury like that. The German shot at me but lost his nerve, and bullets that missed me by a fraction of a centimetre hit 'Majeranek' straight in the head.

The lads stand silent now, knowing how close we were. I take 'Majeranek' in my arms and try to return to the unit with him. I take a few steps and fall. One of the bullets scratched my leg, and I can't stand. The guys take his body, and take me under my armpits, and we return to Nieborów like this. I can't even remember what was done with those two empty tanks.

CONFESSIONS OF A HOME ARMY EXECUTIONER

'Majeranek's' funeral was the only real funeral in which I participated in all of my partisan career. Generally, lads who were lost at a distance from their unit were left or, if conditions allowed, buried on the spot. We had our own cemetery in Nieborów for those who died of their wounds or were killed in action close by. They were buried in just their underwear, because their clothes were often given to a friend who needed them.

A coffin or Mass was out of the question.

But my 'Majeranek' had everything. It was already the fifth year of the war, and German vigilance was much reduced. Besides, our military chaplain, who knew me from childhood, did not dare refuse my requests and arranged everything for me. He even organized a collection for the coffin, which a local carpenter constructed while I waited.

The whole unit of my Second Outpost, apart from officers and lads who were 'protecting' the church during the ceremony, took part in the Mass that took place precisely at midnight at the church in Hyżne. I will never forget that moving moment: the church all lit up, the partisan brotherhood, which after the Mass sang 'God, Thou hast Poland' at the tops of their voices to the accompanying sounds of the organ. […]

I remember how tough I was during those times, but I also remember the tears in my eyes during the funeral. I had gone with this boy on almost every mission. I knew his every move and thought, and I knew I could rely on him unconditionally in any situation. During our free time, we would go out with girls, we drank booze together. We realized that we probably wouldn't survive this war and would have to face the inevitable sooner or later.

4

Operation *Tempest*

O PERATION *BURZA* (*TEMPEST*) BEGAN in the
Rzeszów area on 26 July 1944. [...] People from the
Underground left their homes and families, grabbed any
weapon they could, and joined with the partisans to strike
at the hated enemy with their combined strength. On the
outskirts of villages, barns were turned into 'guardhouses',
where freshly baked 'soldiers' were on guard and underwent
military training.

One such guardhouse was located in Dylągówka. It was the
village where I had spent the lion's share of my younger years;
all the local youth knew me. My mother, who died in 1934, had
her property here. I had come here often, for holidays from
Jasło and from Lwów, where I went to school, and during my
childhood I came here from Nosówka, where I was born and
where my father had a grange. I knew every tree, every hill,
every grove here. I remember how the girls sang to me during
the harvest festival: 'On the Dylągów pond, swans swim free,
our master Stefan a prince shall be.' [...]

[A few days before the start of *Tempest*] I had some spare time, so I decided to visit Dyląg\ówka. I saw around fifteen boys there. Everyone recognized me, so the greetings were heartfelt. A bottle of moonshine was also found. [...]

I am majorly struck by their patriotism. They already feel the end of the war coming; they dream of military actions, of which they know so little and with which they have so little experience. I look at their weapons: not one machine gun, several five-round rifles (carbines) and two small handguns that I would personally be scared to handle. I do not criticize anything, however, as I don't want to spoil the mood and this fighting fervour.

During our conversations, a lad runs into the guardhouse, out of breath. As he was riding through the village on a bicycle, he passed a German heading in our direction, driving a pair of horses harnessed to a large flat wagon. There were many different things on it, certainly looted, and a large Alsatian dog. The German is in civilian clothes; the boy passed him about 2 kilometres from us. He could not see any guards accompanying him.

A great opportunity: the devil knows what might be on that wagon, and the mission looks ridiculously easy. I say I only need one volunteer because taking the whole team for one German is not necessary. The first to volunteer was a lad whose codename I don't remember. I know only that his name was Władek. [...]

We come down from the guardhouse. Władek is armed with

my pistol and I have his carbine; we wait, hidden next to the stream, behind two big trees. The German and the flat wagon do indeed arrive after a few minutes, so we jump out bravely from behind the trees and shout at the top of our throats: '*Halt, Hande hoch!*' [Stop, hands up!] The German stops the trotting horses and lifts up his hands, as per the rules, but the Alsatian riding on the wagon takes a mighty leap and lands on my head, or rather on the barrel of the carbine I am holding. I pull the trigger, and the badly injured dog bounces off my head and falls onto the road with a yelp.

In the confusion, the terrified Władzio shoots the German with the pistol, hitting his neck. Seeing what's happening, the poor little German […] jumps off the platform and starts to run away. He manages to jump over the brook to the other side but slips on some wet grass and falls over.

Władek is the first to catch up to him. He doesn't quite know what to do, because instead of finishing him off so that he wouldn't suffer, he began to check his pockets. He took his personal documents and some rounds for a Soviet machine gun. Meanwhile our little German goes crazy and yells: '*Hilfe, Hilfe, Kameraden, nicht schiessen!*' [Help, help, comrades, don't shoot!]

I can see this is not good. It's all going on in the middle of the main road, so it's not difficult to see it going wrong, especially as German troops escaping the front pass this way every now and then. Standing in the middle, I ask Władzio to move aside a little, as I calmly take the German in my sights and pull the trigger. One shot, and the German stops making a fuss.

Now we grab the horses and pull the wagon to a side road. We have driven maybe 200 metres, when suddenly we hear the sound of an engine, then from around the bend, a truck full of German soldiers appears. We quickly run up a slope without the wagon or the horses, and hide in some bushes. The Germans stop because they saw a corpse near the brook; they begin looking it over but can't make out who it is before them. A guy wearing civilian clothes, no papers, because Władzio has cleaned him out. They either don't see the wagon standing on the side road, or were in such a hurry that they don't want to waste time looking at it. We hear the whirr of the engine. They drive off.

We return to the horses and haul the whole wagon all the way to the guardhouse. Only then do we discover the excellent Soviet machine gun, with ammunition too, lots of brand-new clothes, and the yellow uniform of a colonel of the SA. No wonder the Kraut travelled in civilian clothes. I look through a photo album. A wife and three lovely children to whom he will never return, and an address in Nuremberg. [...]

Meanwhile, there's incredible joy in the guardhouse, the lads share the clothes, and Władek is proud of his first successful mission. Someone pulls out a fresh bottle and, in a happy mood, toasts our successful mission. I return to my unit in Nieborów tipsy, merrily humming under my breath.

OPERATION *TEMPEST*

*

A FEW DAYS LATER, 'Józef', who hadn't been seen in Nieborów for the past month, returned to the unit. After a short greeting, he ordered all officers and senior non-commissioned officers to his quarters. Hanging around for the next three hours, I noticed that nobody moved a step from the building.

Eventually, Lieutenant 'Ryś' appeared and gave the unit its orders: 'Tomorrow at five o'clock in the morning, the entire unit is to gather, not one man can be missing; even those on reconnaissance will be brought down to take part in the briefing. Place: exercise yard, forest clearing Number 3.'

At dawn the next day, we are all at the designated place. Short reports begin. Teams and platoons check in. Finally, 'Józef', the commander himself, appears. I think this is the third time in my life that I have seen him. He is serious, focused and confident. He receives a report from Lieutenant 'Ryś'. He then greets the unit with a few words. He thanks us for our sacrifices and the endurance we have shown over the last years. He also reads out ten codenames for promotion. I hear mine: 'Żbik I'; I automatically take three steps forward. My first promotion in the Home Army. I'm a corporal now. […]

Then the main part of the meeting. I can hear 'Józef's' calm voice: 'Soldiers, we are coming to the last operation of the war, an operation that will bring us the final defeat of the enemy and will clear the way to a free Poland! This operation will be called *Tempest*.'

'Józef' speaks briefly, in military terms. We now all have to walk around with a red and white armband on our left arm, and only Home Army soldiers with these armbands will be respected by the Soviet troops that enter Polish territory. We are to capture all Germans fleeing the front. Our unit must occupy all roads east of Rzeszów. The Wehrmacht will be disarmed and – after receiving special passes – directed towards the Soviets, who will take the Germans prisoner. However, any members of the German authorities (SS, SA, Gestapo, gendarmerie) will be liquidated by us on the spot. [...] Each unit must be in constant contact with the central command.

Cooperation with the local Underground, which is now officially under our organization and which will now directly help us in military actions, is also discussed. Finally, the briefing ends, we sing and then go to our quarters to begin final preparations for the march out to our positions, at dawn the next day.

I returned to my quarters with a gloomy face. I had no confidence in collective action. There would be new faces, new people that would be difficult for me to rely on. I was an expert on individual missions; I had a lot of experience. And here, everything had to start from scratch. I sat motionless by a window for a whole hour, studying the situation. I came to the conclusion that I couldn't smash my head through a wall, that this final mission was unavoidable.

Finally, resigned, I set about cleaning the machine gun and pistol and counting the ammunition. At the end of the evening, I devoured half a bottle of moonshine and fell asleep like a pig, fully clothed, waiting for a better tomorrow.

*

THE NEXT DAY I get to the gathering point by nine in the morning. Borek Stary is about 10 kilometres from Nieborów. There are five of us lads together – luckily, all from my team. We have even managed to bring the only heavy machine gun in our unit, an old Polish Maxim. We settle down about 50 metres from the main Rzeszów road, hidden in a small trench that we dug in the ground, and wait for the Krauts.

After an hour or so, an ash-coloured Mercedes comes around the bend. We take it in our sights and wait for it to enter our line of fire. We have some bad luck in that a peasant and wagon were coming the other way. The Krauts in the Mercedes can't see us, but the peasant notices us immediately. He assesses the situation at once and reins in the horses, obviously in hope of getting to the other side of the road. Our desperate signals for him to stop the ponies don't help; the peasant finds himself right in front of us at the moment the Germans drive by. We have to give up the ambush, and that beautiful Mercedes disappears in clouds of dust in seconds.

A lovely black Opel approaches. This time the road is empty. It drives up majestically in front of our position. I see four people in German uniforms. 'Now!' I shout, and an avalanche of fire streaks towards the car! We shoot at the height of the windows. The Opel, now slowed down, makes a slight left turn and falls into the ditch. I noticed the back door opening seconds earlier, from which a wounded German jumped out onto the road. He tries to get up, but at that moment, a short burst from our heavy machine gun calms him down forever.

We approach the car. All fat cats – a Wehrmacht general among them – what a success! To have proof, I take their papers, even though they are heavily soaked in blood. In fact, there's blood everywhere – on the seats, on the floor, even on what remained of the broken windows. We put the German we killed on the road in the car, withdraw to a safe place, then one of the lads throws a grenade under the back of the car. A powerful explosion and the entire Opel is engulfed in flames. This action is over; we move to our next position and wait for more victims. […]

Our group of five had our hands full with work over the next five days. […] We destroyed about twenty vehicles and killed about twenty Germans, most of them officers.

We also escorted three cars that were still roadworthy to Nieborów. They were fitted with white and red flags on their bumpers, but were unfortunately of highly questionable value to us. The flags weren't visible at night, and when we drove from outpost to outpost – without lights on so as not to attract attention – it was easy to pay with your life, being shot by our own patrols that mistook our cars as being hostile. I tried such a drive just once, and decided that using my own legs was much safer.

We also benefited during these offensive actions when it came to weapons and ammunition. [...] I now have brand-new officer boots and pants. Pockets full of occupation zlotys and cigarettes – I don't smoke rollups any more. However, our fatigue increases after five days of jumping from mission to mission; I'm completely mentally exhausted. My comrades don't look any better. [...] Finally, we return to our beloved Nieborów and ask for two days' rest.

*

AFTER RECEIVING PERMISSION, I rush to my old quarters in the attic and sleep well on the hay for the next twelve hours. It's good that I at least had enough time to take off my boots and give my blisters a rest.

When I woke up the next day, my hostess was already pottering around the room, getting breakfast ready for the 'poor' partisan. My first hot food in five days. Out there on the road, we only ate sandwiches that were brought to us by a messenger from the village. [...]

I have just finished breakfast when I hear the sound of artillery from afar. The hostess and I run outside together. You can hear it very clearly now. All over the village, anything that is alive goes outside. Old women cross themselves piously. The

Soviet offensive, of which I've heard so much in recent weeks, is now close to us. Who knows, maybe a few more weeks or even days, and we will be behind the front line, we will be in free Poland!

The artillery doesn't cease for even a moment now. It is with us constantly, sometimes louder, sometimes quieter; it sounds like gentle music heralding the new life of spring, a completely new future.

I meet with Lieutenant 'Ryś' in the evening. I get new orders. One more day of rest, then back to the road. However, not the five of us this time, but the entire platoon. We are to pick up and disarm Germans escaping from the front.

This last rest was beneficial to me. I've always thought of myself as gentle, and was of the opinion that my hands are of better use caressing women rather than carrying a rifle. So, having one more day at my disposal, I spent it in the arms of a local sixteen-year-old, whose name, as far as I remember, was Jasia. A petite, pretty blonde girl.

The entire platoon marches out at dawn the next day. We walk overladen like oxen. Fully armed, even with shovels for digging. We occupy our new position at the intersection of two roads: to Rzeszów, Błażowa, Dynów, and Łańcut, in the vicinity of Dylągówka. [...] Standing at the crossing of these highways, so close to my home, I feel like a hero who had come to defend his estate with his own blood.

We didn't have to wait long for the Germans. The first group appeared on a distant stretch of the highway. There were about thirty of them. They threw down their rifles at the sight of partisans with white and red armbands. Without any orders, they knew immediately what to do. They slowly approached us with their hands held up high. As they got closer, their appearance struck me.

I remembered the arrogant Wehrmacht from 1939 well. At that time, they had handed out coffee and sugar to the locals at the same intersection. They had beautiful, shiny new uniforms and great weapons. I remembered one of them boasting about their wealth in perfect Polish: 'Your Poland had shit-all, and now, under our occupation, you will have everything!'

The same soldiers were now returning from the east. Or rather, their remnants were returning. Incredibly dirty, unshaven, in tattered uniforms, wearing worn-out boots. Their pride had disappeared; you couldn't see the Nazi arrogance on their faces, their faith in victory. Evidently, their only dream now was to save their own lives and return to their families in distant Germany. I wondered what actual percentage of these Germans would see Germany again. Very few, I supposed.

Of that first thirty that now stood before us, only twenty had the so-called *Soldbuch*, military papers, which we checked straight away while searching them. The other ten said theirs were lost during combat. This may have been true in some cases, but what guarantee did we have that they were not party members, disguised in shreds of Wehrmacht uniforms, trying to smuggle themselves to the west?

Not wanting to risk any chances, we tied their hands behind their backs and – walking them into a small grove on the grounds of the Dylągowski grange – we liquidated all ten of them, shooting them in the back of the head. We sometimes undertook such operations several times a day, burying the bodies when there were more of them. There are many such mass graves in today's Poland …

It is different for those soldiers who have their military IDs. We give them specially prepared passes that entitle them to 'safe' conduct to Jawornik Polski, where they will be taken by the Soviet authorities and sent to POW camps in the depths of Russia. […]

I was now quartering in Dylągówka. […] Once, while I was going on a lunch break, I saw a German whom we had checked and let walk on some half an hour earlier, sitting in a deplorable state at the edge of a ditch. The poor man was almost entirely naked. All he had left was the boot on his right foot, which a crowd of villagers was now actually fighting over. They simply robbed him clean, as his uniform and boots were not completely worn out.

My appeals for them to give everything back to him were met with mockery, and then for good measure, one of the villagers pulled off his remaining boot with a swift movement. The whole crowd moved towards the village, still arguing among themselves along the way. And poor Kraut was sitting in front of me dressed as Adam. I found myself in a stupid situation because I didn't know what to do with him.

I couldn't undress, give him my clothes and then go back naked to my quarters. Nor could I allow him to return to Germany, where he would have a chance to say how the people of Poland had treated him. A huge feeling of regret overwhelmed me; for the first time, I was sorry that I had to participate in such a ruthless war. Without a word, I pulled my pistol from my belt and shot the German between the eyes.

It was two o'clock in the afternoon by the time I finally got to my quarters. The cottage owners had already eaten their lunch and were back at work in the field. I found two dumplings with potatoes on a still-warm stove. […] After lunch, a cigarette – that is, some dried-up tobacco rolled in a piece of old newspaper. […]

I started to think about my future. […] The Soviets are close, there are fewer Germans, and the de facto occupation is over. So there will be a free Poland here in a week or two; the day I have dreamed of will come.

And now that everything was so close, I feel dread. Maybe I will have to lay down my arms and become a civilian, and then what? Finish school? Start working honestly for a living? Perhaps the Home Army will even go with the Soviet Army as far as Berlin, but how long will it take? …

*

MY DUTIES ON THE road continued throughout the following weeks. During the first one, we had a lot of work, but by the end of the second week, there were fewer and fewer Germans, so we had a bit more rest. Until, one beautiful dreamlike morning, the first column of Soviet troops appears on the bend of the road from Dynów.

Three huge tanks at the head, followed by lorries full of military, some with artillery attached to the rear. There are also American jeeps with red stars, Studebakers and Soviet ZIS trucks. After a few minutes, the whole column stops in front of our platoon. A Soviet officer jumps out of a jeep, and we embrace him with joy. There is no end to the greetings. The Soviets praise us greatly, and they can't find enough words of gratitude with regard to these territories that they take over from us without a shot being fired. […]

The Soviets did not have their own provisions, so they immediately went to the village in search of breakfast. You could hear the cackling of chickens being chased, the cries of slaughtered cattle and the squealing of pigs. Some peasants, fed up with the times under their previous 'masters', left their homes to greet the soldiers with red banners, but were later profoundly disappointed when their 'allies' robbed them of everything.

My estate in Dylągówka had a beautiful fruit orchard, and I remember how the Soviet troops cleared it of its winter apples, which had only just formed from flowers, within an hour. I was only surprised that the unripe apples didn't make their stomachs explode.

OPERATION *TEMPEST*

After enjoying the sight of our new 'allies', I return with the rest of the unit to Nieborów finally to get some rest and a good night's sleep. For me and my Second Branch of the Home Army Unit in Rzeszów, Operation *Tempest* is over!

5

Under the Soviets

A FTER TWO DAYS OF rest in Nieborów, I received an order from headquarters to deliver an important letter to a Soviet officer quartered in the Dyląków manor. [...] We had three captured German cars in Nieborów, so my friend 'Żurek' [Mieczysław Pitrus] and I decided to start up one of them. We chose an Opel with red seats to impress our 'allies' all the more. [...] We had some spare gas that we'd looted, and after half an hour of work, we managed to start the Opel successfully and departed on a 3-kilometre drive to Dyląkówka.

We reached the round lawn in front of the main manor house after a few minutes. We were greeted very warmly by the Soviet 'welcoming committee'. They surrounded our car on all sides, admiring its shape and, most of all, the red seats. Eventually, their enthusiasm grew to such a climax that they decided to requisition the car for the Red Army. Our explanations that the vehicle was obtained by us, that we needed it to continue moving around the area in order to hit the Germans, and that we had special permission for it from more senior Soviet authorities, were of no use.

The smiles on their faces now disappeared; a few even got me and 'Żurek' from behind and, after twisting our arms, took our pistols. Next, they relieved us of the watches we'd taken from the Germans; thank God they didn't strip us naked! There were so many of them on this lawn that there was no hope of any serious defence. The letter I was about to deliver to the officer was also taken from me, with the promise that they would deliver it to him later. [...]

After this humiliation, I swore bloody revenge on the Soviets – and just waited for an opportunity to fulfil it. For now, we had to keep quiet because orders were given that we were not to touch the Soviets, because they are our allies and liberators.

*

A WEEK AFTER THE misunderstanding at Dylągówka, I was fixing my hostess's fence. A few nails here and there. After finishing the work, I jumped on a borrowed bike and visited my old friend Tadek Rybka in Dylągówka. Turning onto the dirt road, I headed towards Tadek's house, and here, to my surprise, lying stretched out by the ditch, was a Soviet sergeant, snoring away and dreaming the dreams of the righteous.

I softly jumped off the bike and walked over to him on tiptoes. Having made sure that he was definitely asleep, I took out the longest nail I had from my pocket, and without thinking, using the butt of the pistol slammed its full length into the head of the sergeant. The Soviet just sighed slightly and strained in strange twitches that stopped after a while. Without any emotion or scruples, I got back on the bike and continued my journey.

I found Tadek Rybka happy and at home, or rather next to his house. He was sitting under a large lime tree, firmly holding a very round girl called Mela on his lap, kissing her passionately. I liked Tadek very much for his humour and camaraderie. He was 28 years old, much older than me, but that didn't harm our friendship. He held the rank of sergeant with the partisans. [...] I felt a slight distaste seeing him now with that Miss Melania, with whom I had seen him many times before. They're so old, I thought, and yet their heads are filled with such nonsense. After all, kissing and having sex is fine, but only for the young, not for such old people hitting 30.

I liked to talk to him about old times. After an hour or so, we were joined by two new guests, whom Tadzik introduced as buddies from the Underground. A bottle of moonshine was found, first one, then another, and after an hour, we were all on best terms and singing together [...]. I returned to my quarters at Nieborowa the following morning, drunk, like an ungodly creation. [...]

At around noon the next day, Lieutenant 'Ryś' woke me from a deep sleep. He ran into my quarters all het up and, in chaotic words, started to tell me about political-military events. […] Sandomierz is already in Soviet hands, and an uprising has broken out in Warsaw, organized by the Home Army and under the command of General Bor-Komorowski himself. Half of the city is already in the hands of the Home Army; Soviet troops are already in Warsaw's Praga district, and it's only a matter of time before they hit the Germans from the other side. In the meantime, our entire Second 'Józef' Unit is ordered to leave immediately for Warsaw in order to help with the uprising, in cooperation with the Soviets, of course. […]

I listened carefully, not asking for any details. My three years in the Home Army did their work. I learned to keep my mouth shut and not to comment. I was surprised, however, that they still needed our help since the Soviets were already near Praga. […] I didn't try to discuss these matters with Lieutenant 'Ryś'. Ultimately […] the Home Army was now my life and my 'bread and butter'. […]

At that time, I didn't care about my own life, just as I didn't care about the lives of other people. Not having finished school, I was nothing in civilian life, and here in the Home Army, I carried a large gun under my belt and acted like I was a big deal. […] Always, since as far back as I could remember, I was better at shooting than at Latin grammar. I also learned to carry out blindly any orders I was given. […]

*

WE LEAVE FOR WARSAW the next morning, most of the detachment making its way on peasants' carts towards Rzeszów; I could not squeeze into one of the two cars that were still running. […]

Our first group of ten triumphantly reaches 3 Maja Street in Rzeszów, where the Soviets do indeed greet us very warmly. In full view of the local population, they provide us with gasoline, ammunition and provisions, before bidding us goodbye most effusively. Perhaps its only flowers that are missing. We continue our journey. Our next stop is Sandomierz because other roads are impassable. We are happy as we drive, singing at the top of our lungs […]. Until suddenly, 30 kilometres from Sandomierz, in an empty field, a meadow full of machine guns manned by Soviets.

At first, we thought it was just a routine checkpoint. But when we were told to stand with our hands up, we instantly figured out the terrible truth. Any form of resistance was out of the question. One shot and those heavy machine guns would have made mincemeat of us.

Next, we were thoroughly searched. They took off our white and red armbands and, after tying our hands behind our backs, they packed us into a big truck. Two NKVD guards came with us, weapons at the ready to shoot, the tarp was pulled down, and we moved in an unknown direction without a word.

How wonderfully they played us, I thought to myself, without any witnesses, no fuss. Now they'll drive us to a quiet clearing and we'll dig our own graves. […] I remembered shooting people in the same way. I remembered them asking unsuccessfully for their lives to be spared, so now I decided to die bravely, without the slightest request. My only regret was that I had stupidly let myself be disarmed; if I'd still had my pistol, I could shoot myself in the head, then at least I'd avoid the unnecessary physical work of digging the grave.

My musings were unexpectedly cut short when the truck stopped. They ordered us to get out one by one, under the watch of two new NKVD guards. I was fourth to get out and was surprised to notice that instead of being in the woods, we found ourselves in a city. Sandomierz, for sure, I thought. I was separated from my colleagues and led to a small building, where my first interrogation began in a small room on the first floor.

I was interrogated by an old NKVD major, in the presence of two stiffs with rifles. He asked me questions in Russian, and I answered him in Polish; we understood each other perfectly. I gave him my actual codename, but a made-up surname and false rank of private. I only lied on more important issues to avoid getting confused in case I was asked again.

At first, everything was going well, until we got to two points: why I belonged to the Home Army, and not the Polish Workers' Party, and – where precisely in the Rzeszów region was the rest of my unit hiding out.

I tried to explain to him that I had no idea where the rest of my unit was – that they had likely also gone to help Warsaw

– and that I belonged to the Home Army only because the Polish Workers' Party didn't exist in our area. Of course, that wasn't true because we occasionally saw small PWP patrols – and in all cases, we shot them on the spot, strictly following the orders of the Home Army High Command.

After a while, the major realized that he wouldn't get much out of me by being polite, so he nodded to his comrades, one of whom told me to put my hands up, and the other hit me with his full strength with his rifle butt in the area of my kidneys. Everything went black and I fell onto the floor. When I came to my senses, there were more questions, followed by the same treatment. I finally tasted blood in my mouth and passed out.

This time, when I came round, I was sitting in a small windowless basement with just a tiny door. In addition to a small chair – to which I had the pleasure of being tied – there was a big spotlight that shone brightly right into my eyes all night. I was very weak and swollen by now, and there was no question of sleep. I held on with the last of my strength and dreamed of suicide. You felt the light everywhere […].

I spent most of the day tied up like a goat, and was frequently visited by various NKVD agents, who promised me mountains of gold should I manage to recollect anything of my past. They even promised me caviar for dinner, but for the time being they fed me on crackers dipped in water. As I could not recollect anything for three days, I was taken to the major for daily interrogation. This finished as it always did: I got hit in the back with a rifle, and they dragged me to the basement while unconscious, where I slowly recovered after being drenched with cold water.

On the third day, I knew that death was approaching. I was pretty sure that I would not survive the next interrogation. As I walked up the stairs to the major's office, I also felt a certain kind of resignation. But at the same time, I was proud of myself, as I had kept the oath I had given to the Home Army at the outset, that I would not give anyone away, and now I was to die like a soldier for my country. […]

The major was sitting at his desk, quietly smoking a cigarette. I was expecting the usual questions from the previous days, followed by the usual beating with the butt of a rifle. But this time, to my great surprise, everything happened differently. The major ordered the two men who had brought me there out of the room, and to wait outside the door. Then he started from a different angle.

He explained to me that I was still very young, that these interrogations made no sense as they would ultimately beat me to death with their rifle butts. I was to tell him everything about my comrades who had stayed in the woods to save their lives. I agreed with him entirely on the first point, but as for matters related to the rest of my unit, I told him straight away that I could not help with this because after setting off to help Warsaw, I had lost all contact with them.

This approach immediately angered my major. He pulled his TT pistol from its holster and, aiming it straight at my forehead, said he would shoot me like a dog if I didn't start answering at once. However, instead of shooting me, he rose from behind his desk and hit me in the teeth with the butt of the gun. I tasted the now familiar taste of fresh blood in my mouth.

I observe how he sits back at his desk and places his gun in front of him. He then gets up and, without saying a word, hits me in the face with his fist, making my nose bleed this time. He then goes to the other side of the room, looking pensive. Through my swollen eyes, I can see his TT on the desk, two paces in front of me. Apparently, he forgot to put it away. I try to collect my thoughts, as this could be my only chance. I must act fast, and of course I know this gun very well. Bottlenecked cartridges, extremely powerful, a magazine with eight bullets, the ninth in the barrel.

I quickly start working things out. One shot, and the major is on the floor! The two who brought me will rush in, two shots, and they both eat dirt. Then I run out into the corridor. There will be an emergency guard sitting in front of the building; even if there were even two of them, they would quickly fly up the stairs after hearing the shots. I'll be waiting for them, hiding behind the wall. I'll open fire on them once they're halfway up the stairs. As long as I don't miss a shot, that'll be just five rounds of my ammunition. That will leave me four more, in case of any surprises … With a bit of luck, perhaps I'll get to the street. And what do I have to lose if it doesn't work out? I'll save the last bullet for myself, just in case …

And I was just about to grab the gun when some doubts

started to creep in. That an older man, and one with the rank of major of the NKVD, could have done something so foolish as leave a loaded gun right in front of an experienced Home Army member? No, that's probably impossible! I hesitated now. The major must have noticed this because he came up to me again and gave me another good whack, after which he marched off to the other side of the room.

Now I had no doubts about it. That pistol is not loaded, for sure. […] The major returned to his desk and, sitting down, just waved his hand. He now took out the other, loaded, pistol from his pocket and put it into his holster without any ceremony. And he calmly threw the one that was on the desk into the open drawer.

And now a miracle happened! I wasn't beaten any more. I was only asked if, as there was no PWP partisan unit in our area, perhaps I would like to fix old mistakes by signing up to General Berling's Polish Communist Army and contribute to the liberation of my homeland and build a new People's Poland from its ranks.

Apparently, my self-preservation instincts were still working reasonably well because I agreed to do everything without hesitation. I was brought some papers that I signed without argument and without even reading them. Only then did they officially inform me that I currently found myself in Sandomierz, and that from now on, I was assigned to the Second Reserve Infantry Regiment in Rzeszów, where I will be transported at dawn the next day.

UNDER THE SOVIETS

When I found myself in Rzeszów the next day, I couldn't believe that I was still alive. Although I was constantly spitting blood for the next three days, I wasn't too worried about it any more. […]

*

As much as the Soviet Army was worthy of contempt, you could really have a laugh at Berling's Polish Army. I didn't notice much at the beginning as I was so unwell after my ordeal in Sandomierz, but when after three days I slowly began to recover, many strange things caught my eye. First of all, uniforms. My Second Reserve Regiment barracks were located by the river Wisłok in Rzeszów, and at least 2,000 soldiers were quartered there. Yes, these soldiers did have uniforms, or rather parts of them: someone who had uniform pants was missing the top, and whoever had the top part was wearing civilian pants. And almost nobody here owned a pair of boots.

After a week, I found out that there were boots after all, only in insufficient quantity. That is, a platoon consisting of sixty soldiers had one pair of boots. Who should get these boots? This was solved very simply. As each platoon fielded one guard a day to stand in front of the barracks building, that one sentry paraded in smart boots.

My face was puffy and my back was bruised, so I was a guest of the local infirmary during this period. I was allowed to go out into the barracks yard; no duties were obligatory for me.

After I recovered a little, I was summoned to the office of the captain himself, the commander of the First Company. He knew about my past, so he wasn't interested at all in my appearance, but began to ask about my education and professional skills. I couldn't show off either of these, even if I had wanted to, but he was clearly pleased when I told him I had finished a tractor course and that I could drive a car. Given this turn of events, I was immediately assigned to a motorized platoon. There I reported to the lieutenant, who happened to have a jeep for which a driver was needed. After a short practice, I passed an easy test and now had a vehicle under my protection.

I got a short haircut on the same day, as was standard procedure for recruits. The worst thing, however, was sleeping. I didn't sleep a wink during the first night!

I had to sleep with the rest of my new motorized colleagues. Admittedly there was a place to sleep at the back of the garage, but there were no beds or even a bunk. The entire garage was cemented, and we put boards or old, unusable doors on the cement, and this was how we spent the nights there, without even a blanket to cover ourselves. One end of the garage was cordoned off from the men's toilets, which consisted of at least twenty conveniences, with just thin plywood. Literally the entire regiment used this toilet … The smell was in the air on a grand scale, let alone the noise made by these people, fed on peas or beans almost every day.

I didn't have it bad; my job was mostly driving officers by jeep to different places. Most often, we travelled to Lublin, where this new People's Poland's main headquarters was. However, I noticed that I was not trusted too much, because at first I was not allowed to go outside the gate alone, even to get stupid gasoline. But if you're born to be hanged you'll never be drowned.

After three weeks, I was told to go to town for supplies for the company. As every exit through the gates had to be accompanied by relevant documents, I reported to the duty room for the papers that – to my surprise – I received without difficulty this time. Apparently I was finally considered 'one of their own'!

The sentry didn't notice my mocking smile as I walked through the gate in the dark; nor did he see me hitting the gas all the way as I turned onto the Rzeszów bridge. I was finally free! Fate had smiled at me again, as once again I got out of serious trouble. Now – I thought – back to my unit, to the partisans, to continue to fight the enemy, although this time in different uniforms.

A few minutes later, I found myself on Grunwaldzka Street, where my friend had a car workshop. After driving into the courtyard and closing the gate, I explained the situation to him. Without a word of protest, he called the other mechanic, who started to take my jeep apart, right to the last screw.

Ultimately, vehicle parts were in short supply, so no wonder they both looked happy now. They didn't do me any harm either. They gave me some old clothes, a pair of glasses and 3,000 zlotys in cash.

6

Return

I RETURNED TO NIEBORÓW. […] I walked around our
old quarters and found only a few lads there. Only two
from the team that had left with me for Warsaw had survived:
Bronek Pieniowski and Jędrek 'Słowik' (Nightingale). The
rest had disappeared without a trace. […] As we had also lost
Lieutenant 'Ryś', the immediate commander was now my
close friend Tadzik Rząsa, an old partisan with whom I had
even taken part in a few missions. […]

Less than a week after my return, I remember we were
sitting in the quarters of one of my friends, drinking
moonshine as usual, when the topic of conversation suddenly
moved to our future. To my great horror, I realized that many
of the lads believed that our job was done, that it was time
to move to civilian life, finish school and find some honest
work. With our contacts, obtaining false papers would not be
difficult. […] I was understandably worried for my own skin.
As I was so 'exposed' throughout the county of Rzeszów, any
false papers would not have helped me. […]

Our discussion was interrupted by a messenger from Father Ostrowski,* who said that the priest wanted to see me as soon as possible. Father Ostrowski was our military chaplain, and spent almost the entire war in Hyżne, mainly officiating in the curate's house next to the parish church. [...] He was liked by the whole partisan brotherhood for his courage and his hefty dose of youthful humour. I remember him well from the times he sat with us by the fire in the forest, singing melodiously [...].

I had met Father Ostrowski a few months before joining the Home Army. I had been raised in a very religious atmosphere since childhood, and was very involved in the church, went to confession each week, received Holy Communion on the first Friday of every month and often used to serve at Mass – in fact in many cases, for Father Ostrowski. [...]

Later, when I joined the partisans, we were not allowed to go to church for security reasons, but religiosity remained with me for several years. I sometimes silently made deals with God when I went on missions – that if I was lucky and filled the bastard full of lead, then I would be good and clean in thought, speech, and indeed throughout the following week ...

And those songs we were told to sing over and over:

---

* This refers to Fr. Mieczysław Bossowski 'Żbik' (Wildcat), a priest from Hyżne. The last commander of the Home Army Unit in Hyżne (Stanisław Ostrowski, 'Orzel' (Eagle)), lived with Bossowski, pretending to be the priest's brother – this is probably the reason for Stefan mistaking the name.

Horses, charge like the wind, the young uhlan falls in the field, victory burns in his eyes, as he spills his blood for the Fatherland … And in the lilac bushes, where the bower is, a soft cry breaks off, don't wait, girl, the uhlan will not come back to your call … You will find a birch cross in the field, and a grave covered in flowers, it's for the Fatherland, like the border post, your beloved knight is there keeping guard, don't cry, wipe the tears from your face, from his blood you have Poland!

Isn't that beautiful? When this type of song was constantly sung, it's no wonder each of us sought death.

After arriving at the priest's house and providing a short report to Father Ostrowski, I was introduced to two gentlemen who were there. Captain 'Draża' and Lieutenant 'Belabes' [Józef Szajda] – 'This is Corporal "Żbik",' was the short formal introduction by Father Ostrowski. I was also informed that these two gentlemen were the commander and deputy commander of the subversive unit of the Fourteenth Jazłowiecki Lancers Regiment. I found out that the unit had reached the Rzeszów area during Operation *Tempest*, and that it had previously operated only in the areas around Lwów.

They currently found themselves in the same situation as our 'Józef' Unit, so they had decided not to reveal themselves and to continue the fight in the Rzeszów area. Since they were unfamiliar with the region, they needed a local partisan for a guide, so Father Ostrowski recommended me. I was glad to have such a turn of events because I really knew every corner, bush and tree here. […]

It was past midnight when I said goodbye to Father Ostrowski and set off with 'Draża' and 'Belabes' towards Hyżneński's former grange, where the rest of the Lwów Fourteenth were waiting for us. After a short briefing, during which I was presented to the rest of the detachment, we set off that same night. The village of Szklary, located 5 kilometres from Hyżne, was our first stop and my first task in the role of a guide. I led the group through fields, the shortest route, so we were there in just over an hour. […]

There was no way the whole squad could be quartered in the village. I noticed that 'Draża' had his own contacts here, and that he was expected. I was also surprised by the efficiency with which the village administrator distributed the lads around various quarters. He chose hosts whom the war had not yet ruined completely, and who could afford to feed at least one partisan. I was also allocated accommodation here, but couldn't take advantage of it for the first two days because I had to go to the neighbouring village of Harta that same night, practically at daybreak, where the process of accommodating the rest of the unit was repeated.

I immediately saw that 'Draża' was very much liked by all his partisans, and I soon found out that it was for good reason. He was Serb by origin but spoke perfect Polish, though with a slight accent, and in addition to that, he was perfectly acquainted with our situation. […] They all loved him like their own father, a father who, although he led with an iron fist, was always fair and cared about everything. He planned missions carefully and participated in many of them. He was always concerned about the lives of his soldiers, as I was to find out for myself. Now, when I met him, he held the rank of captain, was 32 years of age, tall and handsome. [...]

Shortly after being quartered in Szklary and Harta, we were temporarily under the command of 'Belabes'. It was not the only time when 'Draża' [...] went out into the field. Because he liked me a lot right from the beginning, he often designated me as his cover. However, I had never gone out into the field with him, and his 'trips' were always kept secret. [...]

I spent the first month as a freshly baked soldier of the Fourteenth completely idle. We now had to be on our guard in Szklary so that we would not be discovered, because during one beautiful night, an entire division of the Soviet Army visited our area. It was the army heading to the front, completely uninterested in internal affairs; however, we still had to be very careful so that they would not notice anything suspicious.

In order not to draw attention to ourselves, we pretended to be family members of the local farmers and hung around the farms, cleaning out manure or working in the fields. A Soviet soldier was now quartered with me in my cottage and slept in the attic while I slept on the ottoman in the main room. I hammered a decent nail into the back of the ottoman, which was against the wall, from which my machine gun hung. I kept the rest of the weapons – grenades, pistol and ammunition –

hidden in the bedding. The situation was ultra-comical; every morning, I grabbed a pitchfork and hung around the farm. It would have been unthinkable under the Germans; only such fools as the Soviets could fall for these antics! […]

Once a week, I went to the so-called *chałupki* – to other homes where our boys weren't quartered. There you could happily drink with the Soviet soldiers and, with some luck, buy some weapons or ammunition from them. Trade in vodka was particularly profitable. And for a watch, every Soviet would pull the machine gun from his back and hand it over without hesitation.

After escaping from Berling's Polish Army, I had got a Russian Pepeszka, so at least now I didn't have to worry about ammunition, which could always be looted from the Russians. In any case, I thought the Russian Pepeszka was better than German automatics. It had a greater rate of fire, excellent dispersal and, most importantly, when the 32-round magazines were used, it never jammed and required much less maintenance and cleaning.

And that's how we lived in Szklary throughout October 1944, like in heaven. Even the Soviet quartered in the same house made friends with me, thinking I was the farmer's son. We often played durak (a card game popular in the countryside) in the evenings, spending some fun time together.

However, the tranquillity ended in early November, when our little soldier marched off for more war with the 'Giermaniec'. We were finally alone, so could go into the forest clearings again, sing songs, march and train. Great emphasis was placed on military drill and general combat exercises. [...]

*

AFTER THE SOVIETS HAD left Szklary, my former friend from the Second Outpost, Jędrek 'Słowik' (Nightingale), joined the Fourteenth. [...] We embraced each other heartily, as there were so many memories from our previous unit that connected us, and we went on several missions together. He was an old killer, only his style was different from mine. In these dangerous times, I liked to drink, but I always went to work sober. 'Słowik', however, had the stupid nature that before every action that awaited him, he had to down a couple of large ones 'for courage'. [...]

And drinking in partisan units was strictly forbidden. There was even an unwritten law with 'Draża': 'A bullet in the head for a glass of vodka.' In spite of this, everybody drank, and everyone knew everyone was drinking. To scare us with the death penalty was like frightening a thief with jail.

*

MY FIRST MISSION WITH the Fourteenth completely failed. [...] It started with our intelligence providing the command with information about a young couple who were eagerly communicating various dangerous pieces of information to local Communists. 'Draża' pronounced the death penalty on the couple after conferring for a short while with 'Belabes'. As Jędrek 'Słowik' knew them well, he was ordered to do the job with me and my new colleague from the Fourteenth, 'Luis' [Lucjan Jaśkiewicz] [...]. Everything looked easy when we planned it. A couple of shots to the back of the head and job done.

This was happening in November, so it was no surprise that the fields were sprinkled with light snow, and the frost was biting when we left Szklary on a Saturday afternoon, heading towards Bachorz. The road was not pleasant, so we walked through the fields. In some places the snow was above our ankles, so already after a few kilometres, I felt that my boots were getting wet. 'Luis' and I started to complain that life was miserable, that only dogs could be coaxed from their homes in such weather. 'Słowik' didn't complain; he always drank some moonshine before departing, so now he was warm, cheerful and even whistled something under his breath at times.

When we got to Bachorz late in the evening, we were already so exhausted that we decided to postpone performing the task until the following evening, so that we could gather some strength for the journey back. 'Słowik' himself helped us make this decision, as he said he knew a girl here, so we shouldn't have a hard time finding accommodation. Indeed, everything went smoothly. The girl was found, along with her parents and a sizable cottage.

After an hour, we were well accommodated. There was also a meal on the table, along with a full litre of moonshine. Later on, of course, a few songs in the twilight, and we all went to sleep. 'Luis' and I on the floor, and the brave 'Słowik' got into the girl's bed. It took me quite a long time to fall asleep. First of all, the bed with the girl and 'Słowik' began creaking mercilessly, and secondly, every now and then she shouted: 'Oh Jesus, Jesus, now, now, now!' 'Luis' took it all with stoic calm, but in the end, even he was getting annoyed because he was muttering, 'Why the hell is she so religious …?'

I woke up lacking sleep and in a bad mood, and only felt better at the sight of pork sausage for breakfast. In addition, my wet footwraps had dried in the kitchen, so I had dry feet now. We spent the whole day in 'Słowik's' girl's cottage, not taking one step outside so as not to arouse suspicion in the village.

When it got completely dark, we said a short farewell before slipping out of the cottage for the mission, which was to be undertaken just a few houses away. Like agile cats we moved silently to the house's windows, which were pointed out by 'Słowik'. The lights were on inside, lots of people, some party was being prepared. […]

The group of people didn't scare us as much as the five stout Soviet soldiers sitting on a bench against the wall, with rifles resting next to them. It was no wonder the Home Army command wasn't impressed with Władek (that was the name of our condemned man). In any case, we backed off to consult for a moment. 'Słowik' informed us that although Władzio was sitting in the middle of the room, there was no trace of his fiancée. So that gave us some consternation, as we needed them both for the liquidation. […] Ultimately, we decided to postpone everything for one more day and return to 'Słowik's' girlfriend's place for the night. […]

We were about to leave when we heard the front door opening and someone started walking in our direction. We had been seen near the fence. When the silhouette came in line with our fence, 'Słowik' took one step forward, looked closely at who was approaching and, pushing him with all his strength towards me, shouted, 'Shoot!' at the top of his voice.

I understood what was going on right away. I quickly took aim with the Pepeszka and pulled the trigger … The silence of the night was interrupted by a long burst from the gun … The figure fell to the ground without a word, as if struck by lightning. We were very lucky that out of so many people in the house, it was Mr Władzio who came out and allowed himself so easily to be shot.

We raced up a steep hill, to be as far away as possible from this house containing five well-armed Soviets. We didn't have to wait long for them. Hearing the rumpus in front of the cottage, they ran outside with their rifles and, seeing our silhouettes now far away on the white snow, they opened an intense fire towards us. Luckily they fired from the spot and didn't risk an open attack. […]

We reached the top of the hill after a few more minutes, where there were a couple of lonely cottages. And here the strangest thing happened. A woman ran out from one of the huts and, coming towards us, started screaming in a desperate voice: 'Władek, where are you? Władek, is that you? What's going on out there?' And so, shouting like that, she reached us.

Despite the night, our faces were clearly visible as there was snow everywhere. I saw how she calmed down a bit when she saw 'Słowik'. 'Jędrek, what are you doing here?' she asked, with a slight trace of fear in her voice. She did not receive an answer, however. 'Słowik' put the gun to her head without a word and pulled the trigger. She fell to the ground and I, firmly convinced that this was Władek's condemned fiancée, also let out a short burst from my Pepeszka. The shots faded away and you could only hear the sound of crying coming from far away. It started to snow as we got to the border of the Szklarski forest, and from there, back to our quarters.

After two days, I found myself at a briefing for the part of the unit that was accommodated in Szklary. Lieutenant 'Belabes' gives orders to the unit commanders: 'On Friday, we're all temporarily moving to Piątkowo, in order to regroup our unit better. We must leave Szklary, especially now after the unsuccessful liquidation in Bachorz.' My ears pricked up. How was it 'unsuccessful?' I wondered. After all, everything went smoothly.

After the briefing was over, I asked 'Belabes' for an explanation. Only then did I understand it all. Władek was executed according to the rules, but the girl wasn't Władek's fiancée at all, but his sister. [...] So why did she die? There was only one explanation. 'Słowik' knew both girls personally, and they knew him. […] He couldn't allow Władek's sister to tell everyone in the village who shot her brother, so he simply shot her in the head so there would be no witnesses.

I find this incident very tragic: the girl that was killed was said to be very much liked in the village, and did not agree with her brother's views; she even warned him several times not to get involved in political matters that could ultimately end tragically. And that's exactly how they ended, also for her. She lost her young life. Completely unnecessarily. But back then, you thought differently. Anyone who dies, dies for their Motherland. That's how we were brought up.

*

IN PIĄTKOWO, MY SOCIAL life was arranged rather well. My quarters were in the neighbourhood of two great boys, 'Przytulski' and 'Ucho'. 'Przytulski' was short, thin and frail, not much good with a gun, but he was a notorious ladies' man, so I liked to go out with him 'for girls'. As he wasn't particularly intelligent, and his body and height also left much to be desired, I was surprised by his remarkable success with women. A certain Helenka explained everything to me in her own way: 'Perhaps there is a shepherd's head, but underneath, there's something else!'

'Ucho', like 'Przytulski', did not go on liquidations and was much less interested in the fairer sex. Instead, he had no equal when it came to drinking: he could drink for two. I liked him very much, as there were never enough friends with whom to drink 'water from the mad cow'. He had a fantastic voice, knew a lot of songs and could sing for hours.

The Fourteenth had so many talented youths. Each of these boys had some speciality and was useful for something. There was a great camaraderie between us, which I think could only have been created to such a degree through life in the forest. Nobody on earth could have fun like our partisan brotherhood. Sometimes food was scarce, but never vodka.

When you visited farmers in the countryside, they didn't offer us any food; at most a piece of dry bread might land on the table, but a bottle of something homemade was always found. There was generally just one glass. According to established tradition, the host took the first drink to prove to the guests that it wasn't some kind of denatured alcohol that could blind you, but solid homemade vodka, of which the farm could be proud. To prove its strength, he often took a lit match in his hand and touched it to some vodka poured on a spoon, which would immediately be set alight with a light blue flame. This was the final proof that his vodka was first-class. After a few 'large ones', the participants' eyes started glazing and the mighty roars of the first songs began to fill the room. It usually started politely. Then came the turn of the not-so-decent songs.

By the end, the songs started to be really offensive, directed at the unseen enemy, and these had to be supported more than once by force of fire. The brotherhood would then draw guns and, to the horror of the hosts and local guests, start to shoot into the ceiling, making the plaster fall from the ceiling onto the heads of those gathered there. The shooting usually began way after midnight, when my friends were really plastered, so nobody dared to protest.

*

IT IS A SAD fact that after the Soviets entered, there were individuals in the villages that not only joined the militia, but also joined the party – from conviction, or wanting to reach higher positions. [...] This 'national participation in political life' began with assisting in the liquidations of various 'reactionary and capitalist elements'. The latter, of course, also included the Home Army, though I swear I didn't have a dime to my name at the time – I was as poor as a church mouse. However, you had to defend yourself against such 'comrades', and the best defence was to slam their heads straight away, before they gained more strength.

Our commander 'Draża' also knew this, and when he was informed of three such gentlemen who lived in Borek Stary, who constantly attended various Communist rallies and events, and went to party member conferences in Rzeszów, only later to incite local people, he pronounced death sentences on them without ceremony.

I went on this mission with 'Luis' and 'Szofer' (Chauffeur) [Feliks Maziarski], and I had to bring three of 'Draża's' boys, who'd just joined the detachment recently, very late on. […] 'Luis' and 'Szofer' hit the liquor in order to gain strength for the evening as soon as we reached the quarters just before sunset. […] When it got dark, we got on with the liquidation. […]

We took the first two men with us without any difficulties. Seeing the secret police uniforms (that we were wearing) through the windows, they let us in without resistance, and they also easily swallowed our story that they had to go with us immediately to Rzeszów on an important matter. The trouble only began with the third, most important, 'comrade'. According to his wife, who opened the door for us, 'he was not at home'.

And maybe the guy could have saved his own life, as we were about to leave, but then the 'comrade's' wife asked us if we had any codeword. Of course, fearing liquidation, her husband had an arrangement with the secret police, whereby whenever anyone had any business with him, they would use a special codeword. Her question buried him immediately. It meant that hubby was only hidden somewhere nearby. There was no other option …

We all took out our guns, and while 'Szofer' and 'Luis' held the two men we had brought with us in check, I put my pistol to the woman's head and, holding a watch, gave her three minutes to show her husband's hideout. Once I started counting the last seconds out loud, she cried out and started calling to her husband, who was hidden deep in the straw in the attic: 'Ah, Wojtek, come down here, because these bastards really will kill me!' Immediately the straw in the attic moved, and the homeowner showed up on the ladder.

We take all the men to nearby trenches that were dug by the Germans. We line up the convicted men one next to the other on the embankment. 'Szofer' and I shoot them in the back of the head from a distance of a few centimetres, he the one to the left, I the one to the right. We fired at the 'comrade' in the middle almost simultaneously. That was our biggest fish!

*

I HAVE ALWAYS BEEN a perfectionist in all my endeavours, whether in sports or at work. I've always tried to be at the forefront. And I was no different in the Home Army. I took my tasks seriously, and – being a specialist in executing people – I carried out the sentences that were ordered without emotion, with stoic calm, glad that I was needed. I realized that without people like me, our Underground could not exist.

But it so happened that even types like me have been on missions that aroused great remorse, and memories of which haunted me for years. […]

In December 1944, about two weeks before Christmas, I received an order from Lieutenant 'Belabes' himself to go as cover for our nurse 'Nuśka' to the village of Borek Stary, where a liaison officer would be waiting for reports from another unit. […] 'Nuśka' and I set off briskly towards Borek in the early afternoon, not expecting any unpleasantness along the way.

I armed myself only with my beloved pistol and two spare magazines in my pocket. We passed through Hyżne in the evening, when it was already getting dark, so we decided to visit Father Ostrowski at his vicarage by the cemetery. We were sure of an hour's rest and some hot tea.

We did indeed find Father Ostrowski at the vicarage, and this time he was also not alone. Four guests sat fully armed at the table, having a lively discussion amongst themselves, while leaning over some papers. I recognized one of them and was glad to see him. This was Tadzik Rząsa, my former buddy from the 'Józef' partisan unit. We greeted each other heartily. 'Nuśka' was also warmly welcomed, and when after a moment, warm tea hit the table, our moods improved a hundredfold.

Father Ostrowski was patting me somehow especially cordially, each time repeating: 'I think that God Himself has sent you to me here this evening.' Finally, seeing my confusion, he explained what was happening. There had been a huge exposure [of Home Army members] in the village of Hyżne. At a militia station half a kilometre from the vicarage, there was a long list of as many as ninety people who belonged to the Underground during the German occupation. In just a few hours, the Rzeszów secret police were to start conducting arrests according to this list. [...]

And now the worst thing. The list was signed by one of the newly baked militiamen, who himself had belonged to the Home Army during the German occupation and knew everybody in the area well. What had got into his head, that he should become a Communist and sell out all his friends, I do not know to this day. This boy was just under 19 years old, he was my age. I'd known him since I was a child. He was one of the few village kids my parents allowed me to play with. We had played football together on a round lawn in Dylągówka, him in midfield and me in right attack. […]

And now, Father Ostrowski is standing before me, asking me to go along with the partisans that are present and shoot my former friend in the head. I try to excuse myself, explaining that I am escorting 'Nuśka', who isn't armed and is taking important reports to Borek. Nothing helps. Father Ostrowski, being a military chaplain, has the rank of captain, and now he simply gives us orders. He takes full responsibility on himself. He will send someone to escort 'Nuśka' and will keep me for this mission, because only Tadzik Rząsa and I have experience of this type of actions. There's nothing doing. 'Nuśka' leaves with a lad from the local partisans, and I lean down over the papers to study the plan of the attack on the Hyżne militia station.

The situation is not easy. Only four of us will go on the mission, as one lad has to give me his machine gun, so he would be left without a weapon. There are seventeen militiamen at the station. Only four are to be shot dead: the very dangerous lieutenant – the commander of the unit – his deputy who holds the rank of sergeant, my former friend Staszek P. and another Communist militiaman without rank. The rest of the militiamen will be on our side and will go with us to 'Draża' after we take the station. […]

After agreeing on the plan, right down to the smallest details, we said goodbye to the priest at precisely eleven o'clock and left. We were already there after fifteen minutes, and without a word, like ghosts, we took our positions at the front door. Although the building was quite impressive – it consisted of a ground floor (which even had prison cells) and a first floor – it was built of wood, so we took off our boots so as not to make lots of noise as we sneaked up the stairs to the upper floor. The first fifteen minutes passed in utter silence; everything was going according to plan so far.

At half past eleven, someone suddenly comes down the stairs. Creak, creak, creak … he goes to the door. It can't be our liaison 'Moris', because he was supposed to come down at exactly twelve o'clock! So what the hell? The two local guys don't wait any longer: 'We've been given away, it's the lieutenant!' And they disappear into the dark night. I am left alone with Tadzik Rząsa. We both have far too much partisan training to run away upon encountering the first problem.

We just lurk like two tigers ready to pounce, and wait to see what would happen next. A few more seconds and the main door opens, and some character leans out. We grab him by the throat, pull him out in front of the building, put a machine gun to his head, and whisper in his ear to introduce himself in a whisper, otherwise we'll fill him full of lead. 'Guys, it's me, "Moris".'

The situation was finally clear. After the militiamen went for a rest, 'Moris's' nerves couldn't stand it, and he wanted to make sure that everything was going according to plan; because of his curiosity, he went downstairs half an hour early. I was angry with him because this was a reckless move – it cost us two lads, and although apparently not too brave, we would have had two more machine guns on a difficult mission. I decided to carry out the mission, even though I knew I had little chance of success. [...]

I was dog-tired after the half-day march from Piątkowo to Hyżne, my boots were soaked and I was hungry as hell because I'd only drunk tea in the vicarage, and lice were eating us alive as usual ... Tadzik Rząsa didn't seem in any better condition, because in answer to my question: 'So, what, are we going in?' he just nodded and muttered under his breath: 'What does it matter, if not today, then tomorrow ...' [...].

It's as dark as down a well inside, and we do everything by touch. There's a long staircase, and we're finally on the first floor. I'm guiding Tadzik and 'Moris' to the end of a long corridor, where the militiamen's dorm was located. I indicate with my fingers for them to give me a minute to get to the lieutenant's bedroom, after which I open the right door, behind which, according to our plan, should be a kitchen. It is indeed there. There's a bed in the corner on which the young cook is sleeping. There's a kerosene lamp on the table. I take it, turn it right up, pass the kitchen, and creep into the lieutenant's bedroom.

RETURN

I barely have time to put the lamp on the table before the lieutenant, who is asleep on a bed in the corner, wakes up (apparently from the bright light) and – seeing me in the middle of the room – tries to grab the machine gun that is lying on the pillow above his head. The reactions of the newly awakened person aren't very fast, however – I smash the butt of my gun on his head in one movement, and then, jumping on his bed, throw him onto the floor.

He collapses like a sack of potatoes; he looks funny in his nightgown and with his white cap on his head. Not knowing what was going on, he immediately starts to create a rumpus, hoping to wake the sleeping militiamen on the other side of the corridor. 'Help, help! What do you want from me? I am innocent!' Then after a minute, the door opens, and the convicted militiamen enter, flanked by Tadzik and 'Moris'. There is a sergeant, a militiaman without a rank whose name I do not remember, and – yes – there is also my childhood friend, Staszek P. He recognizes me straight away. He doesn't say a word to me, but he turns as pale as a ghost. […]

The hardest part of the mission is already behind us. A big success, considering that we have taken the whole station with three people, and without a shot. We do not expect the militia from Rzeszów before five o'clock in the morning, by which time we will be a long way away. I keep all the prisoners under guard, and the rest of 'our' militiamen plunder the entire station along with Tadzik, looking for the unfortunate list. They find it in the lieutenant's desk drawer, along with other documents. Father Ostrowski knew what he was talking about: it was indeed signed by Staszek P., who created the list. Unfortunately, I now have no doubts as to his guilt.

All the papers, important and unimportant, are placed in the middle of the floor, and we make a small, controlled fire. We don't want to burn down the building as other homes are close by, so the whole village could go up in smoke. After the papers, it's the turn of weapons, with which we're not thrilled. Mostly old-fashioned rifles. Only two machine guns, one was the lieutenant's, and the other belonged to the sergeant. We empty the cartridges out of the rifles that were standing in racks, and hang them around the condemned men's necks. [...]

Now we bring this entire group down to the ground floor. We open the prison cell doors with the keys found in the lieutenant's desk and let out the two occupants. Their faces light up when they learn of the burned papers. They are older than us, likely arrested for drunkenness or making moonshine. After two hours of plundering the station, we leave the building. We head towards the ravine by the river, as these were the instructions I received from Father Ostrowski.

The lieutenant's mouth now doesn't shut up. He knows only too well that the end is near, so he does his best to try to save himself. He explains to me that he doesn't know anything about any list or arrests (which betrays him, as I didn't ask about any list), and that he himself is a member of the Home Army. Only Staszek P. hasn't spoken a word so far, walking semiconscious with fear. I feel terribly sorry for him and move to the left side so that Staszek is now guarded by Tadzik. It's a moonless night, and I delude myself, hoping he will perhaps vanish into the bushes before Tadzik's bullets reach him. But no, he goes quietly, as if a happy tomorrow awaits him.

On the other hand, the sergeant, who was now walking with the lieutenant on my side, unexpectedly notifies me that he has to empty his bladder. I moronically stop the whole column and when one of 'our' policemen comes up to us, the sergeant darts into the bushes and tries to get through to the other side of the ditch. But the three rifles he is carrying around his neck slow him down a bit, so that my Pepeszka bullets reach him before he jumps out of the bushes. I was shooting blindly in the dark, and 'Moris' reports the outcome to me only after finding the body.

Another half a kilometre, and we bring the other three to the planned place. We tell 'Moris' to wait at the edge of the field with the rest of the militiamen, while Tadzik and I take those sentenced to the centre of the field. The lieutenant is on the left, Staszek P. is in the middle, and the militiaman is on the right. We order them to stop, remove the rifles from around their necks and lay them down in the snow. They obey the order without objection, but as soon as they put their rifles on the ground, they make a run for it. The lieutenant to the left, the militiaman to the right, and Staszek straight ahead.

I took out the lieutenant with one burst, then turned to the right and helped Tadzik take out the militiaman, although he was not in my line of fire. I was hoping that perhaps Staszek

P. would manage to get out of this mess, and through no fault of my own. But no, instead of fleeing to the left together with the lieutenant, where there were bushes, he was hammering through the centre of the field and was clearly visible in the white snow. I couldn't wait any longer. I aimed the machine gun's barrel towards the fleeing figure and pulled the trigger. A long burst, and I watched in horror as the dark figure fell to the ground. I went to Staszek lying on the snow, to check if he was still alive. He spoke to me for the first time that terrible evening: 'Stefan, finish me off ...'

And then, for the first time in years, I, a tough partisan, had tears in my eyes. I turned to Tadzik, who was standing to my side a few steps away from me: 'Tadzik, help me ...' He understood, walked over to Staszek without a word, and when I had turned my back to him and started leaving, heard one last short burst. As I exited the field, I passed two people from the village, sent with shovels by Father Ostrowski; I pointed to where the bodies lay.

After a short farewell to Tadzik, who was returning to the vicarage, I left with 'Moris' and the rest of the militiamen to Piątkowo and to 'Draża'. I didn't speak a word throughout the entire journey back. I had begun to realize for the first time that maybe this partisan war was a lost cause, and that these sacrifices and tragedies didn't make much sense.

7

Ukrainians

I DON'T KNOW WHO hated whom more: Ukrainians Poles, or Poles Ukrainians. In any case, 'Draża' hated them, and so did the entire Fourteenth. And for good reason.

The Fourteenth was formed in Lwów, and although it consisted mainly of Polish members, it was nonetheless surrounded by Ukrainian villages. When I attended the Abrahamowicz school in Lwów in 1939, I didn't hear much about Ukrainians, and the issue was rarely raised. Big problems only began with them after the outbreak of the Soviet–German war. The Ukrainian Insurgent Army, which – having opted for the German side – vigorously set about the liquidation of Polish citizens. […]

The attacks by Ukrainians on Polish villages were terrible. […] They rarely used a pistol or machine gun; most of the victims fell from their knives or axes. […] Women and children were slaughtered just like the men. They took Polish babies by the feet and smashed their little heads against the wall. [...] Clearly, in 1943, there was no option other than a robust retaliation from the Polish Underground.

The Fourteenth was one of the first units to act against the Ukrainians. [...] Ukrainian villages were burned down, without sparing anybody. 'Szołomyja went up in flames ...' – went a song of the Fourteenth. Yes, Szołomyja was one of our greatest victories. One of the main Ukrainian headquarters went up in smoke. [...]

The situation in the vicinity of Przemyśl or Przeworsk was truly tragic. Many villages in these areas consisted of a mixed population. For example, the upper part of the village was made up of Poles, and the lower part was Ukrainian. There was seldom a week where we did not hear about an attack by Ukrainians on Poles, murdering them mercilessly, to the last. The Ukrainian Insurgent Army existed here, just like in the good old days near Lwów, with the only difference being that it did not have any support at that moment, either from the Germans, because they were now fighting for their own skins near Berlin, let alone from the Soviets.

After my return from Hyżne, I got new lodgings, this time in Laskówka. From there, three days before Christmas Day, I saw a huge glow in the sky. This was one of the Polish villages being put to the torch by the Ukrainians. The glow was visible throughout the night, and when we got there the next day, we found people arranging their murdered countryfolk in rows on the grass. They prepared them for a mass burial. A truly horrible sight, and the worst for me was seeing brutally murdered little children.

My friend from the Fourteenth, 'Twardy' (Strong) [Wilhelm Ćwiok], who lived with his brother in Pasieki in Lwów, had his entire family – father, mother and siblings – murdered by Ukrainians. Although he and his brother survived, neither of them could ever forget this tragedy, and finally, 'Twardy's' brother shot himself at a dance, in front of his girlfriend and other friends. 'Twardy' also had suicidal tendencies, and you had to keep an eye on him when he drank vodka, so that he didn't put a bullet in his own head.

This same 'Twardy', whose second pseudonym was 'Wiluśko' […] was assigned by 'Draża' himself with me, 'Słowik' and 'Luis' to a special punishment unit, set up for retaliatory liquidation of Ukrainians. This was our regular everyday work. 'Szofer' and 'Muszka' (Fly) joined us on larger operations.

Our operations were similar to the Ukrainian ones, with the only difference being that we chose villages in which the Polish population predominated because that way it was easier for us to finish off the Ukrainians. There was no mercy during these operations, no pardons. I couldn't complain about my own companions in arms. 'Twardy', especially, having personal scores to settle with the Ukrainians, exceeded himself. As we entered a Ukrainian house, our 'Wiluśko' literally went into a frenzy. Built like a well-developed gorilla, as soon as he saw Ukrainians, his eyes bulged, saliva dripped from his open mouth, he gave the impression of a man gone mad.

'Luis' and I usually covered the doors and windows, while the almost insensible 'Twardy', an old cutler from Pasieki in Lwów, threw himself at the petrified Ukrainians and cut them to pieces. With incredible skill, he ripped open their bellies or slit their throats until blood spurted across the walls. Amazingly, instead of using a knife, 'Twardy' often used an ordinary table bench, with which he shattered skulls as if they were poppy seeds.

*

ONE TIME WE GOT three Ukrainian families in one house, and 'Twardy' decided to finish them off 'cheerfully'. He put on a hat he'd found on a shelf and – taking a violin that was lying on the table – started playing to the Ukrainians. He divided them into four groups and made them sing in harmony to the sound of a tune: 'Here's a mountain, there's a valley, and Ukraine will be deep in shit ...' And under threat of the pistol I was holding, the poor souls sang until the panes of the windows trembled, deluding themselves that our partisan brotherhood would have a greater conscience than them. Unfortunately, it was their last song in that valley. After the concert, 'Twardy' got to work so energetically that both 'Luis' and I fled into the hallway so that he wouldn't mistakenly chop us up. [...]

*

UKRAINIANS

THE LOCAL CITIZENS' MILITIA also helped us with liquidating Ukrainians. We had one of our 'own' outposts located near Dynów, close to the river San, which helped us by simply handing over for shooting Ukrainians who had been arrested as suspects for burning down Polish villages. Instead of taking them to the main command centre or the courts, they let us know via a messenger that such and such a Ukrainian was waiting for us at the police station, and was to be collected. Then, there was work for only me and 'Twardy'.

We mainly went to pick up in the evenings, then a drive to the river. Here we put the guy onto a promontory, and to be certain, we filled him with machine-gun bullets, so that an already-dead body rolled into the water. [...] 'Majestic corpses' developed from these bodies, which only surfaced after a week. They floated downstream, swollen as if they were pregnant, bruised, and full of holes. [...]

When I remember it today, I feel a great disgust within myself. But back then, it was different – looking at those bodies, I thought I was a hero who was working hard for the Fatherland, and who was only admiring the fruits of his work. [...] We killed about fifty Ukrainians collected from the police station.

*

SOMETIMES THINGS HAPPENED IN the Underground that even I didn't like. Okay, sometimes during the war, it was

101

necessary to put a woman against the wall and execute her for some sort of treason. I took part in such liquidations myself, and I have no complaints about that; back then, I considered it something necessary, something normal. But 'Twardy' loved torturing Ukrainians, and women were no exception.

One time, walking through a village with 'Twardy' and 'Luis', we entered a house where three girls lived. During the conversation, it turned out that one of these girls was Ukrainian. As she was very young and very pretty, 'Twardy' decided that the best punishment for her Ukrainian descent would be for all three of us to rape her. I was unpleasantly surprised by this idea, but I didn't give that away because there's nothing worse for a 19-year-old boy than to admit that he is 'afraid of ass'. Nobody protested, and the girl was taken to a separate bedroom, where the first alone with her was the originator of the idea, Corporal 'Twardy'. He came back after ten minutes, sweating like a mouse, and 'Luis' took his place. Finally, it was my turn.

Upon entering the bedroom, I found the poor girl lying completely naked on the bed and sobbing hysterically. I felt stupid and genuinely started feeling sorry for her and didn't know what to do. Finally, I sat on the edge of the bed and began gently stroking her long, black velvet-like hair. I started asking her to stop crying, and I even tried to tell her that maybe everything would end well, though in the depths of my soul, and knowing 'Twardy' well, I knew what the end would be like. Still, I felt terrible. The girl was beautiful and still so young, and she certainly hadn't hurt anyone in her life and had the same right to life as each of us. The fact was that she was unlucky to be born Ukrainian – because of that, her fate was already sealed.

I was too engrossed in my partisan career and 'patriotism' back then to go out and tell 'Twardy' right to his face that we were being pigs and that this girl should be acquitted. I had the same military rank as 'Twardy', so there was no question of me giving any orders. Except my way of thinking back then was so skewed … I thought the first step to heroism was to be tough, like 'Twardy'. Following this rule, I did not think seriously about saving the girl.

I didn't rape her as the third, that's true, but mainly because rape didn't excite me, and a girl's hysterical crying would put me in a depressed mood. Having messed up my hair accordingly, I went back into the room, out of breath and wiping sweat from my dry forehead, where meanwhile, my colleagues were having fun talking to the two Polish women. I stated that I was 'sorted' and that I was putting the girl at 'Twardy's' disposal, but with a slight suggestion to spare her life. 'Twardy', although looking at me as if I was crazy, agreed to it unexpectedly easily, although stating: 'You, "Żbik", always have idiotic ideas.'

However, the rape itself was not the end of the ordeal, and although 'Twardy' did indeed spare her life, he first pulled her naked into the kitchen and, heating up a poker, branded her bare bottom so that red stripes began to show.

And, in such a state and completely naked, he threw the poor girl outside. She saved her life with her last remnants of strength, running to her neighbours in icy frost and snow up to her knees.

*

AFTER THIS INCIDENT WITH the girl, I came to the conclusion that 'Twardy' had an exceptionally good 'nose' for Ukrainians. After all, he had recognized that girl immediately, even though she lived with two Polish women. Another incident convinced me of his talent two days later.

When we were returning to our quarters at Laskówka that evening, he accosted a stranger who was calmly walking past, and asked the guy if, by chance he wasn't Ukrainian. He, albeit speaking with a bit of a strange accent, declared with gusto: 'I, gentlemen, am Greek Catholic, I'm not Ukrainian!' 'Twardy', however, refusing to give up, asked me to cover the guy with my pistol while he, taking the belt off his trousers, began to pound him mercilessly in the face.

At first, the poor man even started to protest and shout about what kind of order we were keeping, that we are attacking him when he is not a Ukrainian, but a Greek Catholic. Yet 'Twardy' mercilessly hit him, harder and harder. In the end, the pain was apparently unbearable, because suddenly, the guy – jumping up on one leg, like a wounded hare – agreed with us about everything: 'Yes, I am Ukrainian, I am a motherfucker

…' At this point, the interrogation was over, and the sentence was carried out by 'Twardy', who skilfully slit the condemned man's throat.

*

THESE VARIOUS 'HEROIC' FEATS of ours were noticed in smaller Ukrainian agglomerations and, fearing ever greater repression from us, the Ukrainians quietened down a bit. During the first two weeks of January 1945, not one Polish village was attacked. It was some kind of progress for sure. Our acts, however, were not liked by the Ukrainians, who began to set up special alarm posts in some mixed villages, whose purpose was to check the ID cards of individual Polish passers-by. Generally, such one-man posts were located on the main highways, near a small cottage, which was transformed into a guardhouse. As these posts were new to me, it is no wonder I almost paid with my life during my first confrontation with one.

It started with the fact that 'Słowik' and I were invited to a wedding in Gulcowa. The reception was going to be fantastic. I left my usual pistol at my quarters and borrowed a little one from platoon leader 'Józef', a little 6 mm that was easy to carry in your pocket, allowing for more freedom of movement. I didn't have too much faith in the little gun's firepower, but not foreseeing any military clash, I felt it was pointless to burden myself unnecessarily.

Sitting with 'Słowik' as guests of honour, we poured full glasses of moonshine into ourselves. I sang merrily at the top of my voice: 'Fuck you Kaśka, I'll say this to your face, because I tried you for nearly a month at your place ...' I also picked myself up from the chair from time to time, to dance the polka with a country girl. 'Słowik' was too busy with the bottles even to think about dancing. The party was coming to an end at around three in the morning, and the time came for us to return to our quarters. It wasn't easy, considering we had come here on bikes borrowed in Laskówka. We finally got on the bikes with great difficulty after a few attempts, and – weaving across the road – moved forward.

Humming merrily under our breaths, we'd almost arrived at Jawornik, when suddenly, on an empty road, a figure with a long rifle loomed and, stopping my slow-moving bicycle, shouted: 'Stop! Who goes there?! Papers!' I could tell he's a Ukrainian by the accent. 'Słowik', although not knowing what was going on, had also luckily stopped and was acting calmly for now. The Ukrainian was now the master of the situation; he kept me covered with his rifle aimed straight at my chest.

I began to negotiate with him, explaining that I'd forgotten to bring my papers with me, that I lived in a neighbouring village, and that I was coming back home from a wedding ... the Ukrainian was listening to my reasoning calmly, but did not move the barrel of his rifle from me. And I don't know how it would have all ended if not for 'Słowik', who unexpectedly joined the conversation: 'What the hell is going on, and why the fuck are we standing here? … And who's this?' – the Ukrainian became concerned and instinctively shifted the barrel of his rifle from me to 'Słowik'. I was waiting for this moment. In a flash, I grabbed the gun by the barrel and pulled it towards the ground. The Ukrainian, who had kept his finger on the trigger, pulled it at that point. A bang from the shot, a clang from a bicycle, and 'Słowik' fell to the ground. 'He's killed my friend,' I thought.

Furious and having completely sobered up, I take out the little 6 mm from my pocket and, still holding the rifle with one hand, I fire into the dark towards the Ukrainian with my second. Bang, bang, bang – I hit the Ukrainian with my 6 mm, and nothing; he's still standing bravely on his feet. I fired maybe five times until the Ukrainian cried out: 'Gentlemen, enough now …'. I understood immediately that things were not good, that I would run out of bullets if I continued to miss, as I think I only had two left. Fortunately, I managed to find his head with the tiny barrel and fired for the sixth time. This time my Ukrainian immediately calmed down and fell onto the road. I guess all this happened in the space of a minute.

I ran over to 'Słowik', who – surprisingly – was not only alive, but didn't even have a scratch on him. When the Ukrainian fired, although no bullet hit him, the extremely drunk 'Słowik' fell onto the road with his bike. Now, still not understanding anything, he kept asking about some shooting nearby. What trouble I now had, trying to get him back onto his bike and continue our journey. We had barely reached the first corner when I heard loud male voices. It was not hard to guess that the guards from the guardhouse had stumbled upon the body of their colleague.

8

The Fiołek Family

THE FIOŁEK FAMILY LIVED in Wesoła. It was a large village, with over 900 people. It was split into two main parts: upper and lower. As with every village of this size, it had a steward, a *sołtys** and its own administration. This administration did not like the Fiołeks. And it had good reason. The Fiołeks didn't work the fields, didn't go to church, were not interested in any internal village politics, did not attend any meetings or assemblies, nor did they work physically for their daily bread. They just lived off theft and robberies from Polish citizens. It made no difference to them if it was a church, a rectory or the farm of a more affluent peasant.

The Germans could not deal with them, and it was also somewhat difficult for our militia to tackle them. Either there were no witnesses or no evidence in court, and they were

---

* A *sołtys* is the elected head of a *sołectwo*, whose duties are to represent it and organize village meetings, introduce new laws that have been passed, collect taxes and participate in council meetings.

always ordered to be set free. Many of their robberies were blamed on the Home Army, which especially hurt as, while we took everything from those sentenced to death, innocent Polish citizens and of course churches were never touched.

Finally, it had come to the point where the local militia of Wesoła had reached an understanding with the command of our Fourteenth as to their liquidation. 'Draża' agreed easily because he'd always had our good reputation in mind. Not foreseeing any major difficulties, he appointed me, 'Słowik' and 'Ciuchraj', who was less experienced in liquidations, for the mission. After receiving the order, the three of us reported to the *sołtys* in Wesoła, asking for three separate lodgings in the lower part of the village. We gave ourselves a day of rest, after which we got to tracking down the Fiołeks.

So far, we knew that the family comprised five men who were active gang members, and whom we had orders to eliminate. Three of them were brothers – all ginger. The father, older, was as grey as a pigeon. And one cousin with the surname Dobosz, was chestnut. I spent the whole day in upper Wesoła, asking various farmers for details. Gradually I found out where they lived, where they spent their nights, and where they gathered in the evenings. However, the gang turned out to be better organized than it initially seemed.

The next day, after I said goodbye to 'Słowik' late at night and went to my quarters, there was a bitter frost and snow up to my knees. It was a bright night, a full moon, and when I got to the cottage where I was quartered, I saw clearly the shadow of an individual hidden behind the corner of the house in the snow. I ground to a halt, then instinctively threw myself into the bushes to run away. I had only taken a few steps when a long burst from a machine gun broke the silence of the night. I got to the gully in two jumps and rolled into the stream below like a ball. Burst after burst pounded in my direction. Only enormous luck and intuition saved me from certain death.

'Słowik's' and 'Ciuchraj's' quarters were on the other side of the stream. Both lads were waiting for me with machine guns ready to fire. We ran back to the place from where the shots had come, but found nothing but tracks in the snow. From that moment, however, we stopped underestimating the Fiołeks, who, for the time being, knew more about us than we did about them.

Two days passed and 'Draża' along with 'Belabes' visited us in Wesoła. They walked through our territory and wanted to find out how we were dealing with the Fiołeks. 'Draża' couldn't understand why we hadn't made any progress. He told me that he had some new urgent missions planned for me. I thanked him for thinking of me, and promised to try to end this whole thing as soon as possible.

Meanwhile, the evening had closed in, and because our meeting had lasted late into the night, 'Draża' and 'Belabes' decided to stay the night in Wesoła. The village was constantly under threat from the Fiołeks and, seeing that now two such big fish were supposed to stay here for the night, it went without saying that we decided to arrange first-rate protection for them. 'Słowik's' billet was arranged right next to 'Belabes' and 'Draża's' billets, so we decided to change it into a guardhouse for one night. I assigned 'Słowik' and 'Ciuchraj' the first night patrol, with a change every four hours. As my down time fell right at the beginning, I tried to get my head down, at least for a while. I had taken off one boot and started on the other when out of nowhere, I heard a long burst from a machine gun from very close by. My trained ear immediately recognized the type of weapon. A slow rate of fire – an English Sten. Another second and two quick bursts, this time from a Russian Pepeszka.

Like a madman, I pulled my boot back on and launched myself out as if from a slingshot, pistol in hand, in the direction of the firing. I must have passed four cottages when I saw some figure crouching behind a barn. I fell to the ground next to a tree in the orchard and started crawling on my stomach. 'Get out with your hands up because I'll make a sieve out of you!' I shouted, now afraid to come out into the open.

'Stefek, it's me, "Słowik", don't shoot!' Having recognized him by his voice, I go to him, and now we both go to look for the figure which, according to 'Słowik', opened fire first. And … after just a few steps, we find a seriously wounded 'Ciuchraj' lying on the ground. At that moment, concerned about the shooting, 'Belabes' joins us, revolver in hand. We try to piece everything together – what actually happened. According to 'Słowik's' version, he and 'Ciuchraj' saw a silhouette between the cottages, and when they tried to identify the visitor, he started to run away from them. They then ran in two different directions and by some miracle, ran into each other. According to 'Słowik', 'Ciuchraj' opened fire on him first, apparently thinking he was shooting at the guy who was running away. And that makes sense – the first shots were definitely fired from an English Sten, which 'Ciuchraj' had. Whereas 'Słowik' opened fire – also not knowing who he was shooting at – while defending himself. Either way, 'Ciuchraj' was now lying by my feet on the ground, and I knew he was dying. Shot with just one bullet, but through his stomach, without immediate transport to a hospital, he had no chance. I remember the words he spoke after those unfortunate shots: "'Żbik", it really hurts ...' Then he lost consciousness.

He died an hour later at our quarters, where we'd moved him to after the accident. As the clothes we walked in were almost rags, and 'Ciuchraj' was wearing a half-decent Polish uniform, we carefully undressed him and started to prepare him for an immediate funeral. It did not go smoothly, because there had been a biting frost for a good few days, and the ground everywhere was frozen like stone. And there was no way we could arrange a pickaxe. We packed the poor 'Ciuchraj' on a small child's sleigh and headed to the nearby cemetery, where we wanted to leave him by the cemetery chapel. We managed to get to the place at around two in the morning and, surprisingly, we found a freshly dug grave, apparently prepared for someone else's funeral. Without much thought, we lowered our deceased into the deep grave and, taking off our hats – though the frost was bloody sharp – we said a little prayer.

My thoughts now flew away for a moment to distant Lwów, where I had gone to school before the war, and where during time off from study, I would sneak off to the Uciecha cinema in Mikolasch Passage. Often after leaving the cinema with my buddies, we sang a song [...]. 'Ciuchraj's' father was the owner of this cinema. He probably never learned how pointlessly and unnecessarily his son had ended his life. Straight after the prayer, we slipped out of the empty cemetery like ghosts and returned to guard 'Draża's' quarters.

Although 'Draża' and 'Belabes' left Wesoła the next day, given 'Ciuchraj's' death, I was able to ask 'Draża' for help in liquidating the Fiołeks before he left. He kept his word, as two days later our friend 'Twardy' himself joined us in the company of platoon leader 'Józef', who reported to us the new directives relating to this liquidation.

We received unexpected help from the militia station in Wesoła, which, having had enough of this whole situation, decided to hand over the Fiołeks to us 'to be shot'. The whole Fiołek family was to be taken by the militia for a confrontation with a family that had never been attacked by them – for identification purposes. Not being guilty, the Fiołeks would go with the militia without resistance, and we would nicely take over when they are on their way back.

We were all ready by the evening and set off for the designated position, which was just one house nearer to the cottage appointed by the militia for the confrontation. We arrived at the place just as it was getting dark and waited for our bandits in the hall. Sure enough, at around nine o'clock, the whole gang, accompanied by five militiamen, marched right past the front of the cottage we occupied and headed towards the nearest house. Having spent about fifteen minutes there, they left, and surprisingly – instead of going back down the same snow-trodden path they came by – they trudged off through fields and the largest snowdrifts.

Only their cousin Dobosz, apparently less cautious or braver, decided to return as prescribed. As soon as he came near the porch, he fell into our hands. This is where 'Twardy' started his work, because we needed to hurry and couldn't alert the rest of the Fiołeks with shots. We managed to pull Dobosz inside, but although 'Twardy' had a knife in his hand, Dobosz did not want to allow himself to be slaughtered so easily at all. He started throwing himself around like a young foal, and even bit my hand when I tried to cover his mouth. In addition, he began to yell at the top of his voice: 'By God, help me, they are murdering me here in cold blood, help, help!!!' 'Twardy' didn't give up and – stabbing ceaselessly – finally managed to silence him forever. However, the damage was done. The Fiołeks, having no weapons with them, understood immediately what was happening. Without thinking at all about saving Dobosz, they got on with saving their own skins.

After stabbing Dobosz, we rushed like hungry wolves in pursuit of the rest. It was not easy to catch them up. Snow reached up to our waist in some places, which made the chase extremely difficult. Although we saw their silhouettes clearly in the white snow, they were too far away for an accurate shot from a machine gun that used pistol ammunition. On top of that, we noticed that the distance between us did not decrease by even a step. Every couple of metres we came across pieces of their clothing – here a winter coat, there a hat, here a sweater. Naturally, it was easier for them to escape without being overloaded, but there was no way I was going to take off my winter coat, because what would I wear the next day?

First, we chased them uphill, and then downhill. Eventually, seeing that there were rural cottages nearby, among which the Fiołeks would lose us completely, we opened fire on them out of desperation while in pursuit. One of us got a hit. We reached one Fiołek who was already lying motionless in the snow. Platoon leader 'Józef' let loose a burst from a German automatic into him, now without any reaction from the guy lying there. It was the father of the whole family, who you could immediately recognize by the silver hair. He probably couldn't stand the chase and simply dropped dead from a heart attack. The rest of the Fiołeks, having reached the first houses in the village, completely disappeared from our view.

Angry and disappointed, we returned to Wesoła, unable to forgive ourselves for missing such a fantastic opportunity.

Platoon leader 'Józef' and 'Twardy' left us in the morning the next day, because 'Twardy' had some important mission assigned to him in a Polish-Ukrainian village. I was left alone with 'Słowik'. I was particularly interested in a party which – as I found out – was supposed to take place on Friday, which was that evening.

Driven by intuition rather than reason, I slipped into the orchard well after midnight, and then up to the windows of the homestead from which you could hear the tender sound of a violin being played. And suddenly – I could not believe my eyes – one of the Fiołek brothers was sitting quietly on a bench, right under the window through which I was looking, not sensing anything. Completely ginger, there could be no mistake here. I was only surprised to see that he chose to go out to have fun right after losing his father. Apparently he wasn't very religious, or he didn't especially love his father. In any case, I couldn't miss out on such an opportunity. Having taken out my pistol and flipping the safety, I placed the barrel almost to the glass and pulled the trigger. No longer worrying about the result, of which I was now sure, I jumped off the window sill in one leap and disappeared like smoke into the shadow of the night.

We now had only two Fiołeks left from the whole gang. I must admit one thing about our Home Army partisans: if someone was sentenced to death by us, they almost never escaped with their lives. At that moment, however, neither 'Słowik' nor I knew how to deal with the two remaining Fiołeks. Another day passed with different combinations, but no results. 'Muszka' came to our aid, having been sent by 'Belabes', and brought new information from the police about the time and place of the Fiołek brother's funeral.

This information was enough for us. We watched the funeral from a safe distance, and what's most important – looking at the retinue, we tracked down the house that our Fiołeks now inhabited. In the early evening, all three of us, that's me, 'Słowik' and 'Muszka' who was sent to us, occupied a neighbouring farm – to the dismay of the farmer – and waited for the Fiołeks.

We had their home under constant surveillance, believing that sooner or later, the unsuspecting brothers would go outside and allow themselves to be easily shot. It was barely nine o'clock when we saw a figure walking along the edge of the path leading towards the house we'd surrounded. 'Słowik' kept an eye on the farmers while 'Muszka' and I went outside the cottage with the intention of identifying the stranger. I took maybe two steps, and there's a bang, bang – the figure fires at me from a pistol. I think there were three – fortunately inaccurate – shots in quick succession; he didn't have time for any more. A long burst from my Pepeszka, and he fell to the ground. We cautiously ran closer, there was blood everywhere already. We quickly checked: hair red as hell! Fiołek number four: at his brother's funeral in the morning, dead in the evening.

We had one more left. It was not difficult to guess that he was sitting in that neighbouring house and, though armed to the teeth, knew now that it was no joke with us, and he was undoubtedly meditating how to break out. Meanwhile, in the cottage that we'd occupied, we consulted about our subsequent actions. As the night was moonlit and fresh snow was lying on the ground, the neighbouring house was clearly visible. There was no question of our Fiołek escaping, but we decided to wait with the offensive action until the morning, because storming a defended house is much easier during the day.

At last, the night began to end, and with the dawn, the first fumes coming from chimneys appeared; because it was Sunday morning, the locals were getting ready to go to church. […] The three of us went on the attack. 'Słowik' to the back door, 'Muszka' through the first front window, and me through the second. At my nod and without a word, we open fire with machine guns, shooting full magazines into the middle of inhabited rooms, not worrying about any consequences. I'd already emptied the entire magazine of my Pepeszka when suddenly a boy no more than 11 years old flew through the middle door, pale as a ghost with fear, and began to shout in a frightened voice: 'Gentlemen, stop shooting, there's nobody left alive inside!'

We grabbed him under the armpits and, pushing him forward like a living shield, went inside. In the first room, which served as a kitchen, we saw a terrible sight. In the very centre was the boy's father, with his head almost completely shot off. Not far from him was a pretty 10-year-old girl in a white dress and only one white shoe on her foot – the other was lying nearby, she hadn't yet managed to put it on when 'Muszka's' shots reached her.

The situation in the other room that came under my fire did not look much better. The Fiołek lay shot up like a sieve under the window with a loaded pistol in his hand. We found the farmer's wife badly wounded under the bed, with almost her whole side shot off. Apparently, she jumped under the bed after hearing the first shots in an effort to save her life, but my shots caught her there too. She died from blood loss within fifteen minutes.

We spend about half an hour in the cottage, the boy still sobbing hysterically. We rubbed his temples with cold water, knowing he was in shock, and concerned that he would lose his mind completely. Before leaving, we sent him to a neighbouring house, hoping someone there would take care of him. Observing his departure, it was not difficult for us to notice the faces of scared villagers pressed to the windows. The local population, as always, was at the mercy of people who were participating in the war. They never knew what the future would bring, if tomorrow they would be murdered due to someone else's mistake.

Finally, we departed. We left Wesoła and headed towards our previous quarters. The orders of the Home Army were fulfilled. The Fiołek family had ceased to exist. We carried out this liquidation in the name of the Fatherland …

Maybe I am writing these memoirs too cynically, but – please believe me – I felt terrible then, and even today, I still have a bad taste in my mouth.

9

Exit

THE FACT THAT I eventually emigrated to wealthy America I owe to a certain [Leon] Dobrucki. Who was Mr Dobrucki? An important figure at that time. Everyone knew him, especially in the Rzeszów province and the county of Brzozów. A young, ambitious, high-ranking Communist, the biggest fish after the *starosta*.* […] He constantly went on about how Lwów had never belonged to Poland, that it was the fault of the Polish nobility that blood was constantly and unnecessarily shed for this city! Then he set to parcelling up estates and arresting people for even the most minor offences against the new Communist laws. And so he battled and battled until he finally received the death sentence. The liquidation did not look easy, as he had to be dealt with in broad daylight, in the county's main city. 'Draża' was evidently in a good mood when he signed Dobrucki's sentence because

---

* The *starosta* or *starost* is a term of Slavic origin denoting a community elder whose role was to administer the assets of a clan or family estate.

in one fell swoop, he also added the *starost* of Brzozów [Mambort Orlicki] to the list. […]

'Draża' appointed the liquidation trio himself. Apart from me, Sergeant 'Szofer' and 'Słowik' were also going. As always with such important missions, I was informed about the task in the evening, just before marching out. It was sod's law that – not sensing anything coming up – I had loaned my lovely P38 to someone for another mission, and as a result, I was left without a pistol. Miraculously, I finally managed to borrow an American Smith & Wesson six-shot revolver, a little inaccurate, but still better than a slingshot.

We departed early in the morning […] on 5 March 1945. The march was tiring as there was still a lot of snow. We got to the city at around nine in the morning and looked for the bar where a local contact was waiting for us. The bar was located in front of the *starosta* building, where an important Communist meeting attended by the *starost* and Dobrucki was taking place. For now, we had nothing to do but wait until this meeting was over. […] It finished at around eleven o'clock, by which time I had already drunk four mugs of beer. Lots of people began pouring through the main door of the *starosta* building. Finally, a tall figure in a Soviet cap appeared on the main steps. Our local liaison, who had hitherto watched the building without a word, whispered to us: 'That's Dobrucki, and the one on the right is the *starost* … Good luck!' After these words, he disappeared.

[…] We are in the street now and keep an eye on them. They are surrounded by a large group of militiamen with machine guns hanging from them. For now, we keep a safe distance, waiting for a better opportunity. [...] They walk very slowly, apparently discussing the meeting they've just had between them. We stand in front of the displays, trying to draw as little attention to ourselves as possible. [...] On the way, our gentlemen decide to visit the militia station; they stay there for about four hours, and we – like a bunch of idiots – walk along the opposite side of the street for all that time. [...]

At around five o'clock, the whole group stops at the party canteen for dinner. Twilight is already in full swing. The canteen is located opposite the park, so all three of us hang around there for now. We watch our targets through a large window as they gobble up fried cutlets, and I'm damned hungry here, having had nothing pass my lips since yesterday, apart from some cold beer.

They are in no rush to leave, and I suddenly get cramps in my stomach that are so painful, I can barely stand upright. Finally, what I was most afraid of ... diarrhoea. I rush to the nearest bush every few minutes, and every time it seems to me that I will lose my stomach. I'll need to shoot at people in a few minutes, and here I have to hold my pants with one hand. 'Słowik' and 'Szofer' are also becoming nervous because they were counting on my significant firepower, yet here I am, only making noises in the bushes.

It is probably already seven in the evening when the *starosta* and Dobrucki decide to leave the canteen. Through the window, we see how they pay the bill and leave ... Surprisingly, they are alone this time! Not sensing anything wrong, they head for a side street straight after leaving. [...] The three of us start to follow them. We draw our weapons, 'Szofer' a Polish Vis, 'Słowik' an automatic pistol captured from the Fiołek we'd killed, and I my borrowed revolver. We are some 15 metres behind them, so we increase our pace, because it's a little too far for a shot from small arms in the dark. As the distance between us narrows to ten paces, Dobrucki, who has heard someone following them, is not able to hold his nerve and, poking his friend in the ribs and tossing back his coat, pulls out a brand-new Russian TT and shouts: 'Stop, what is this?!' As the *starosta* has reached into his pocket at that same time, there is no point waiting!

I was in Dobrucki's line of fire; I fired first in his direction and missed. 'Szofer', having the best gun, took out the *starosta* on the spot, but so far only injured him. 'Słowik' tried to fire, but his pistol fell apart [...]. And now all hell broke loose. Standing by the wall of the tenement building, I let the whole drum loose towards Dobrucki, and I could not hit the son of a bitch properly. Admittedly, I managed to smash his knee, but that didn't extinguish his fighting zeal. Kneeling, he shot at me nervously, but thankfully didn't hit me either. Plaster fell on my head because all the bullets that passed me by have hit the house wall. Having fired an entire magazine, Dobrucki loaded another and continued firing in my direction. [...] It looked as if I hit him in the other knee, because he stretched out along the ground, stopped shooting, and began to withdraw on his stomach.

Meanwhile, the wounded *starost*, having been shot in the chest, was lying flat on the ground and loosing an entire magazine in the direction of 'Szofer'. At one point, I hear the words 'He got me.' In truth, it was only in the leg, but right through the centre of the bone and from a high-calibre weapon. Throwing my revolver into a nearby orchard, I grabbed the Vis from 'Szofer' and from two steps, I fired what was probably the last bullet into the head of the *starosta*. [...]

Being faithful to the principle that you do not leave your friends to certain death, we took the wounded 'Szofer' by his arms and dragged him through orchards and gardens, through deep snowdrifts and fences, to just get further away from the militia, which had already organized itself into action and followed us in pursuit. [...] Felek was getting heavier and heavier. I felt that it was only a matter of time before the first Pepeszka bullets reached us. However, a strange incident came to our aid. There was a child's sled with a rope standing quietly by a house we'd passed, ready for the off. We saw our one last chance. Without a second thought, we put Felek on the sled, and 'Słowik' and I, like a pair of racehorses, grabbed the rope and scrambled downhill!

Finally, we managed to get to the main road; sliding along its centre, we obliterated traces of our tracks, which would have been dangerous for us. But the end of our troubles was still far away, because we couldn't run with the wounded Felek forever. Above all, he needed urgent help, and secondly, our strength was already nearly spent, so it was only a matter of time before we fell into the hands of the militiamen who were now chasing us. We needed to take a risk, and to take it immediately.

There was a mighty Jesuit monastery on the right side of the road. We ran through the gate and banged on the front doors with all our strength. They were opened slightly for a moment, and the frightened friar asked us politely about the purpose of our visit. Having learned that we were from the Home Army, he didn't want to hear any further details – and immediately led us to the upper floor [...]. The monks cleaned the wound, applied bandages and even found an anti-tetanus injection. And it was high time. His leg had swollen up like a balloon, and he'd lost a lot of blood. We had to cut his boot open with a knife, otherwise it was impossible to remove it from his leg. As soon as we finished working on the wounded 'Szofer', we heard a knock on the front door. It wasn't hard to guess what the new guests wanted. The militia, not catching us up on the road, now began to search the buildings in the surrounding area. [...] The Jesuits packed us under the beds in their cells. [...]

Though they searched the first floor, the militia did not dare to look in the cells, or were in too much of a hurry. Only after they left did I begin to realize that we did indeed have a chance of getting out of this trouble in one piece [...] We spent the rest of the night with the good Jesuit fathers. The next morning we were offered an excellent breakfast. We'd already started the second day without a spoonful of food in our mouths, so it's hardly surprising that the warm scrambled eggs tasted so good to us. I even forgot about the diarrhoea, with which I'd done battle throughout the whole previous evening. Now even Egyptian cigarettes made from pre-war tobacco were found. In the end, the kind fathers arranged a cart with a horse for our Felek and transported him to a hospital – not the one in Brzozowski, of course – where he spent some three months before returning to his unit fully recovered, just limping slightly.

I found out later from people who read a description of our action in the *Gazeta Brzozowska* that the *starost* was killed on the spot, while Dobrucki was taken to hospital, as he was found seriously injured and in critical condition. [...] As I'd spent a good few hours in the bar, someone recognized me, and my description was in the newspaper. I was already wanted for desertion from the army, and now I also had murder pinned on me. I was sentenced to death in absentia, and they started looking for me in such a way that [...] I found myself in the first group of ten to go to the West.

*

WHEN YOU HAVE SHOT at someone who speaks the same language as you, at someone that you have perhaps known for years, it is somehow difficult to square that with your conscience. In the name of what, and what prompted us to commit acts that the civilized world almost equated with murder? Was it done 'in the name of the Fatherland', or was it in the so-called scope of wartime activities?

It was our duty to listen blindly, connected with innate patriotism. It was our duty to show the world that a Pole will never give up and will die with a smile on his face, 'for your freedom and ours'. But often, in reality, while he was alive, he murdered all who were not on his side or disagreed with his ideas – with the full approval of our command.

I realize that reading this could make the reader shake their head in disbelief and accuse me of gross exaggeration. That's understandable when you bear in mind that no participant in the partisan war has written anything on this topic. Nobody today wants to take responsibility for the complete failure of our wartime actions; today's 'activists' prefer to falsify history and whitewash everything in an unbelievable way, rather than shed light on real events and warn future generations before they commit similar mistakes.

You can draw conclusions from history and learn something, as long as everything is based on the truth. Therefore, in this book, I only write about wartime actions in which I directly participated. I do not write about things that I was told, or that I did not witness. I provide facts from the life of a simple Home Army soldier.

For years after the end of the war, I tried to analyse myself and ultimately found that I had reached this animal-like state mainly through my upbringing during my youth – in an atmosphere of patriotic extremism. Each of us is born like a simple stone that can be cut to your liking. Each of us, regardless of nationality, is the same. When you instil into a child from the cradle onwards how important the Fatherland is, that you must fight your enemy until victory or death, then that child – when it grows up – will fight when ordered, and shoot at anyone who has different views, or is of a different nationality.

Writing these recollections today, I try to justify my actions, and of those people like me, when it comes to the huge wrongs we did to the human race. It's too late today to ask anyone for forgiveness, and people wouldn't get their lives back anyway. Let it be one more warning to future generations and various political players. Let them remember that every war is a tragedy, that young people who have their whole lives ahead of them always die in them – and they die unnecessarily.